A Simply Delicious Christmas

Second Edition

D1005320

By the same author

Simply Delicious
Simply Delicious 2
Simply Delicious Fish
Simply Delicious in France & Italy
Darina Allen's Simply Delicious Recipes
Simply Delicious Food for Family & Friends
Simply Delicious Versatile Vegetables
Simply Delicious Meals in Minutes
A Year at Ballymaloe
Irish Traditional Cooking
Ballymaloe Cookery Course

A Simply Delicious Christmas

Second Edition

Darina Allen

Gill & Macmillan

Gill & Macmillan Ltd
Hume Avenue, Park West
Dublin 12
with associated companies throughout the world
www.gillmacmillan.ie
First published jointly with RTÉ in 1989
First published in this format 2002
© Darina Allen 1989, 1991, 2002
0 7171 3503 9
Photographs by Kevin Dunne
Food styling by Rory O'Connor
Design by Slick Fish Design
Print origination by Carole Lynch
Printed by GraphyCems Ltd, Spain

This book is typeset in Trade Gothic 9 on 12pt.

The paper used in this book is made from the wood pulp of managed forests. For every tree felled, at least one tree is planted, thereby renewing natural resources.

All rights reserved. No part of this publication may be copied, reproduced or transmitted in any form or by any means, without permission of the publishers.

5 4 3 2

For my mother Elizabeth O'Connell
and
my mother-in-law Myrtle Allen
with love

Contents

EDIBLE PRESENTS   **81**

INDEX   **102**

‡ = May be prepared ahead and freezes well
* = Keeps at least a week and in some cases for longer, but doesn't need to be frozen

Foreword

In *A Simply Delicious Christmas* there are lots of favourite Christmas recipes. Some are easy and take just a few minutes to prepare; others are more elaborate, involve a little bit more time and could be served for a special occasion. The whole purpose of the book is to try to make life easier for everyone during the festive season. Christmas can be such a happy and carefree time for some families and such a total disaster for others. Each year the commercial side seems to gather momentum and the real meaning of Christmas is sadly over-shadowed. It can be a time of great joy when families, neighbours and friends get together and take time to stop and chat and share; instead for some it's an endless round of parties, over-eating and sore heads, while for others it's a time when their lack of resources seem even more acute. Every time they turn on the TV or radio or look through a paper or magazine, there's another glitzy temptation which serves to remind them further of what they can't afford for themselves and their children. Some can resist temptation, others borrow wildly and so it takes months of even greater deprivation to get straight again. This year let's have a real Christmas: let's stop the mindless excess, stop the endless merry-go-round of present giving — so many people get so many presents they don't need or want, while others have nothing. This Christmas let's stop and think!

My happiest Christmas memories were of Christmas at Belmont, an old rambling house where we lived for some time. We had several Christmases when the whole family gathered together from home and abroad; we would drive up from Cork on Christmas Eve and usually arrive in time for supper. As we drove up we could see the Christmas candle twinkling in the windows, an old custom to guide the Virgin and Joseph through the night. Mummy always had the house so beautiful: copper and brass shining; a huge Christmas tree with candles as well as tiny fairy lights; and fires everywhere, not only in the kitchen and drawingroom, but also in our bedrooms. We usually had scalloped potato for supper, a layered potato dish with little bits of beef and kidney in it, which we all loved from childhood and 'ordered' in advance every time we were coming home. After supper which we ate in the huge kitchen, we would go up to the drawingroom, which was quite a way and necessitated darting up an icy cold corridor. All the rooms were warm, so we would run from one end of the corridor to the other; sometimes in really cold weather there would be ice on the inside of the windows! In the drawingroom we would all sit round the fire and have tea and cut the Christmas cake.

Then the children were dispatched to bed because Santa mustn't catch them awake and we spent our time catching up on each other's lives and doing last-minute present wrapping. Some went to Midnight Mass. Santa came to everyone, little and large, so there was great excitement on Christmas morning. We had a huge breakfast, then Christmas dinner was usually eaten at about 3 or 3.30 p.m. in the dining-room; again a large fire and the table beautifully laid; usually grape and melon with mint, a wonderful turkey with all the trimmings, Mummy's plum pudding and also a trifle — we always ate both, plum pudding on very hot plates first and then trifle later.

After all the clearing up, usually done by the boys, we sat around the fire in the drawingroom again and exchanged presents — quite a lengthy business in a family of nine children and many grandchildren! In the evening my aunt and uncle and their family usually arrived; more tea, turkey sandwiches and games; and then tired but happy to bed.

On St Stephen's Day traditionally everyone went to 'the hunt', either in Johnstown or Abbeyleix, and followed the action for most of the afternoon, depending on weather. We usually ended up in a pub — Morrisseys in Abbeyleix was a favourite haunt.

The whole secret of Christmas it seems to me is to get the entire family involved right from the beginning of December; it's just an attitude of mind, nothing to do with being wealthy or poor. All the family can have fun sitting round the fire, planning and making home-made presents and cards which mean so much more than expensive baubles bought in desperation at the last minute.

The aim of this book is to help everyone to have lots of fun preparing for Christmas; it's such a shame that many people feel so overwhelmed by the extra volume of cooking that by the time Christmas Day comes they couldn't care less if they never got a bit to eat and just wish to goodness the whole thing was over. Well, it need not be like that. First and foremost, don't be brainwashed by tempting advertisements into buying or making more than you need for your family and friends. I often think (except I never manage to do it myself) that the ideal thing to do would be to sit quietly by the fire one evening in November before the Christmas panic sets in, make out a list of what actually has to be done and then put realistic dates beside it.

Prepare as much as possible ahead of time. The Christmas Cake, Plum Pudding and Mincemeat may be made well in advance and left to mature. Christmas Biscuits could be made over a period of weeks, perhaps at the beginning of December, and stored in airtight tins. Thinking along these lines, we have decided to indicate by symbols which recipes may be prepared ahead and stored or frozen without deteriorating, so that you can have a frazzle-free Christmas.

There are also lots of recipes for using up the 'left-over' bits in delicious ways. In addition, I have included a wonderful recipe for a Christmas dinner complete in a dish: Turkey and Ham sandwiched together with Mushrooms à la Crème, potatoes piped around the edge — and the whole thing can be frozen. The aim of this book is to help everyone to glide through the extra cooking so they actually enjoy Christmas!

Acknowledgments

So many people have helped me to put this book together. First I would like to thank Myrtle Allen for her inspiration and generosity to me over the years and in particular for permission to reproduce many recipes from the Ballymaloe repertoire. I would also like to thank my husband Tim who supports me through thick and thin, my totally unflappable head teacher Florrie Bolger and our assistants Susie, Annette and Fionnuala who tested recipes until they were ready to scream! My secretaries Rosalie Dunne and Kitty Daly who typed and retyped recipes, often late into the night, while struggling with a new and sometimes temperamental word processor. And last but certainly not least D Rennison Kunz: she is the real reason my books make it to the publishers just in the nick of time; she actually gets on a train and comes down after me, locking me into a room until I come up with the goods — for which I am eventually truly grateful! Also a special thank-you to Rory O'Connell for food styling and Kevin Dunne and his assistants for wonderful atmospheric Christmas photos — taken on blisteringly hot days in June! And thanks also to Irene Bauer and Elsa Schiller for sharing their recipes with us and for giving permission to reproduce them in this book.

Glossary

Bain-marie (or water bath): Can be any deep container, half-filled with hot water, in which delicate foods, e.g. custards or fish mousses, are cooked in their moulds or terrines. The bain-marie is put into a low or moderate oven and the food is protected from direct heat by the gentle, steamy atmosphere, without risk of curdling. The term bain-marie is also used for a similar container which will hold several pans to keep soups, vegetables or stews warm during restaurant service.

Bouquet garni: A small bunch of fresh herbs used to flavour stews, casseroles, stocks or soups, usually consisting of parsley stalks, a sprig of thyme, perhaps a bay-leaf and an outside stalk of celery. Remove before serving.

Cling-film (or 'Saran Wrap' as it is called in the United States): Used for sealing food from the air. Use 'pure' cling-film or 'Glad Wrap'. Cling-film containing PVC is considered harmful in contact with food.

Concassé: Concassé means roughly chopped, usually applied to tomatoes. Pour boiling water over the very firm, ripe tomatoes, leave for 10 seconds, then pour off the water. Peel off the skin, cut in half, remove the seeds with a teaspoon or melon-baller, cut into quarters and chop into 5 mm (¼ inch) or 3 mm (⅛ inch) dice. Concassé may be added to a sauce or used as a garnish.

Creamy milk: When one of our recipes calls for creamy milk, we mean a mixture of one-third cream to two-thirds milk, or even one-quarter cream to three-quarters. Creamy milk is often used in soups or sauces when full cream would be too rich.

De-glaze: After meat has been sautéed or roasted, the pan or roasting dish is de-greased and then a liquid is poured into the pan to dissolve the coagulated and caramelised pan juices. This is the basis of many sauces and gravies. The liquid could be water, stock or alcohol, e.g. wine or brandy.

De-grease: To remove surplus fat from a liquid or a pan, either by pouring off or by skimming the surface with a spoon.

Egg wash: A raw egg beaten with a pinch of salt, it is brushed on raw tarts, pies, buns and biscuits to give them a shiny, golden glaze when cooked.

Julienne: A term used when vegetables or citrus fruit rinds are cut into very fine, thin matchsticks or 'needle-shreds'. A recipe will sometimes indicate the size required. Generally a julienne of vegetables or citrus fruit rind is used as a garnish, but sometimes a much larger julienne may be used as a vegetable or as part of a salad.

Macerate: To soak fruit in syrup or other liquid so that it will absorb flavour and in some cases become more tender.

Mandolin: A kitchen implement made of stainless steel or wood, with adjustable blades used for slicing vegetables into various shapes.

Palette knife: A useful but not essential piece of kitchen equipment, it is a blunt knife with a rounded tip, and a flexible blade useful for spreading meringue, icing, etc.

Paper lid: When we are sweating vegetables for the base of a soup or stew, we quite often cover them with a butter wrapper or a lid made from greaseproof paper which fits the saucepan exactly. This keeps in the steam and helps to sweat the vegetables.

Roux: Equal quantities of butter and flour cooked together for 2 minutes over a gentle heat. This mixture may be whisked into boiling liquid to thicken, e.g. gravies, sauces, milk etc.

Silicone paper: A non-stick parchment paper which is widely used for lining baking trays, cake tins etc. It may be used several times over and is particularly useful when making meringues or chocolates, because they simply peel off the paper. 'Bakewell' is the brand name; it is available in most supermarkets and newsagents.

(To) Sponge: A term used when working with powdered gelatine. The gelatine is sprinkled over a specified amount of liquid and left to sit for 4–5 minutes. During this period, the gelatine soaks up the water and becomes 'spongy' in texture — hence the term. Gelatine is easier to dissolve if it is sponged before melting.

Sweat: To cook vegetables in a little fat or oil over a gentle heat in a covered saucepan, until they are almost soft but not coloured.

Vanilla sugar: We store our vanilla pods in castor sugar. Gradually the sugar becomes impregnated with the flavour of vanilla, the sugar is then used for biscuits, cakes and puddings where vanilla flavour is desirable.

N.B. All Imperial spoon measurements in this book are rounded measurements unless the recipe states otherwise. All American spoon measurements are level.

Starters

Because it's winter we've got lots of lovely warming soups in this section all of which may be made ahead and even frozen if you like. Don't forget to freeze some in single portions, for example in yoghurt cartons, so that they can be easily and quickly defrosted if a child runs in cold and hungry. With a nice slice of fresh soda bread it's a meal in itself. Some are made with cheap and readily available ingredients, others with slightly more unusual vegetables such as the maddeningly knobbly Jerusalem Artichokes or Celeriac. Jerusalem Artichokes are well worth growing if you have a spare spot in your vegetable garden; once planted they re-emerge every year and are marvellous for soups, vegetable and gratins. You can just plant the ones you buy in the shop if you are wondering about where to get seed. The Turkey Broth is made with the turkey stock made from the left-over carcass and giblets; make sure it's reduced enough so it has plenty of flavour, and garnish with a fine julienne of vegetables. The turkey liver can be used to make a delicious smooth pâté which will be a great stand-by in your fridge or freezer. The Smoked Salmon starters are light and very stylish; remember to use good quality Smoked Irish Salmon; if you make it with the 'bargain' stuff you'll wonder why you bothered! Native Irish Oysters, the best oysters in the world, are just the thing for a celebration. All they need is a little squeeze of lemon juice — don't dream of ruining them with Tabasco or horseradish sauce. Some people are squeamish about eating raw oysters, but do try again, suddenly you'll find you're hooked!

Fruit starters are just perfect before the robust rich meals of winter. For Grape and Melon with Mint choose the best melons you can find and take the time to peel and pip the grapes; the flavour is immeasurably better if you do and think of how aghast you friends will be when they discover that you spent the afternoon peeling and pipping grapes — it's worth a good half-an-hour's slagging at a dinner party! Pomegranates are in the shops for a short period just over Christmas, into early January; they are hard on the outside and full of rose-coloured juicy seeds in the centre. They are quite often eaten in the Middle East sprinkled with rosewater but teamed up with segments of pink grapefruit they make a deliciously refreshing and sophisticated starter.

Winter Leek and Potato Soup
SERVES 6

55 g (2 ozs/½ stick) butter
110 g (4 ozs/1 cup) onions, peeled and cut into 5 mm (¼ inch) dice
140 g (5 ozs/1 cup) potatoes, peeled and cut into 5 mm (¼ inch) dice
340 g (12 ozs/3 cups) white part of leeks, sliced
1.1 L (2 pints/5 cups) home-made chicken stock
salt and freshly-ground pepper
55–115 ml (2–4 fl ozs/¼–½ cup) cream *or* creamy milk to taste

Garnish
a blob of whipped cream (optional)
finely-chopped chives

Melt the butter in a heavy saucepan; when it foams, add the potatoes, onions and leeks and turn them in the butter until well coated. Sprinkle with salt and freshly-ground pepper. Cover with a paper lid (to keep in the steam) and the saucepan lid, and sweat on a gentle heat for 10 minutes, or until the vegetables are soft but not coloured. Discard the paper lid. Add the stock; boil until the vegetables are just cooked. Do not overcook or the vegetables will lose their flavour. Liquidise until smooth and silky, taste and adjust the seasoning. Add cream or creamy milk to taste.

Garnish with a blob of cream and some finely-chopped chives.

Carrot and Parsnip Soup
SERVES 6

30 g (1 oz/¼ stick) butter
110 g (4 ozs/1 cup) onions, peeled and cut into 5 mm (¼ inch) dice
140 g (5 ozs/1 cup) potatoes, peeled and cut into 5 mm (¼ inch) dice
255 g (9 ozs/2 cups) carrots, peeled and cut into 5 mm (¼ inch) dice
125 g (4½ ozs/1 cup) parsnips, peeled and cut into 5 mm (¼ inch) dice
850 ml–1.1 L (1½–2 pints/2½–5 cups) home-made chicken stock
salt and freshly-ground pepper
dash of cream *or* some creamy milk (optional)

Garnish
chopped parsley

Melt the butter in a heavy saucepan; when it foams, add the potatoes and onions and turn them in the butter until well coated. Sprinkle with salt and freshly-ground pepper. Cover with a paper lid (to keep in the steam) and the saucepan lid, and sweat on a gentle heat for 5 minutes. Add the carrots and parsnips and sweat for a further 5 minutes. Discard the paper lid. Add the stock, bring it to the boil and simmer until the vegetables are just soft. Be careful not to overcook it. Liquidise or put through a mouli or use a Braun Multipractic hand blender. Taste and add a dash of cream or creamy milk and more seasoning if necessary.

Serve sprinkled with chopped parsley and for a special occasion, a tiny blob of whipped cream.

Celeriac and Hazelnut Soup

SERVES 6

Celeriac is a relatively new vegetable in our shops; it is in fact a root celery which looks a bit like a muddy turnip. Peel it thickly and use for soups or in salads, or just as a vegetable.

425 g (15 ozs/3 cups) celeriac, cut into 5 mm (¼ inch) dice
110 g (4 ozs/1 cup) onions, cut into 5 mm (¼ inch) dice
140 g (5 ozs/1 cup) potatoes, cut into 5 mm (¼ inch) dice
45–55 g (1½–2 ozs/¼–½ stick) butter
1.1 L (2 pints/5 cups) home-made chicken stock
salt and freshly-ground pepper
115–225 ml (4–8 fl ozs /½–1 cup) creamy milk (optional)

Garnish
2 tablesp. hazelnuts, skinned, toasted and chopped
a few tablesp. whipped cream
sprigs of fresh chervil *or* flat parsley

Melt the butter in a heavy saucepan; when it foams, add the potatoes and onions and toss them in the butter until evenly coated. Season with salt and freshly-ground pepper. Cover with a paper lid (to keep in the steam) and the saucepan lid, and sweat over a gentle heat for about 10 minutes, until the vegetables are soft but not coloured. Discard the paper lid. Add the celeriac and chicken stock and cook until the celeriac is soft, about 8–10 minutes. Liquidise the soup; add a little more stock or creamy milk to thin to the required consistency. Taste and correct the seasoning.

To prepare the hazelnuts: Put the hazelnuts into a hot oven, 230°C/450°F/regulo 8, on a baking sheet for about 10–15 minutes, until the skins loosen. Remove the skins by rubbing the nuts in the corner of a tea-towel. If they are not sufficiently toasted, return them to the oven until they become golden brown. Chop and keep aside to garnish.

Serve the soup piping hot with a little blob of whipped cream on top. Sprinkle with the chopped hazelnuts and a sprig of chervil or flat parsley.

Jerusalem Artichoke Soup with Croûtons
SERVES 4 APPROX.

Jerusalem artichokes are a very neglected winter vegetable. They look like knobbly potatoes and are a nuisance to peel, but if they are very fresh you can sometimes get away with just giving them a good scrub. They can be served not only as a vegetable but are also delicious in soups and gratins.

225 g (8 ozs/1½ cups) Jerusalem artichokes
110 g (4 ozs/1 cup) onions, peeled and chopped
30 g (1 oz/¼ stick) butter
570 ml (1 pint/2½ cups) light-coloured chicken stock
225 ml (8 fl ozs/1 cup) approx. creamy milk
salt and freshly-ground pepper

Garnish
freshly-chopped parsley
crisp, golden croûtons

Melt the butter in a heavy-bottomed saucepan, add the chopped onions and artichokes, cover and sweat gently for 10 minutes approx. Add the stock and cook until the vegetables are soft. Liquidise and return to the heat. Thin to the required flavour and consistency with creamy milk, and adjust the seasoning.

Serve in soup bowls or in a soup tureen. Garnish with chopped parsley and crisp, golden croûtons.

Croûtons
SERVES 4

1 slice of slightly stale pan bread, 5 mm (¼ inch) thick
15 g (½ oz) butter
1 tablesp. (3 American teasp.) olive oil

First cut the crusts off the bread, next cut into 5 mm (¼ inch) strips and then into exact cubes (a cube is a six-sided square with equal sides).

Melt the butter in a clean frying pan with the olive oil. Turn up the heat and add the croutons. The pan should be quite hot at first, then reduce the heat to medium and *keep tossing all the time* until the croutons are golden brown all over. Drain on kitchen paper.

Note: Croûtons may be made several hours ahead or even a day ahead. Any oil could be used and the oil could be flavoured with rosemary, thyme or onion.

Turkey Broth with a Julienne of Vegetables
SERVES 6

This delicious soup is based on stock made from a turkey carcass. If the stock tastes weak, just put it into a wide saucepan and reduce it *without a lid* until the flavour has concentrated sufficiently.

1.1 L (2 pints/5 cups) well-flavoured home-made Turkey Stock (fat free)
55 g (2 ozs/scant ½ cup) carrots, cut in fine julienne strips
55 g (2 ozs) leeks, cut in fine julienne strips
55 g (2 ozs/scant 1 cup) small button mushrooms, thinly sliced
285 ml (½ pint/1¼ cups) home-made Turkey Stock
15 g (1 tablesp./4 American teasp.) chopped scallions *or* spring onions, cut diagonally

Bring the 285 ml (½ pint/1¼ cups) of turkey stock to the boil, add the julienne of carrot and simmer for 5 minutes. Then add the leeks, season with salt and freshly-ground pepper and simmer for a further 3 or 4 minutes, or until both vegetables are tender (the carrots should still have a slight bite). Drain and keep aside until needed.

Just before serving: Bring the well-flavoured broth to the boil, season with salt and pepper, add the julienne of vegetables, finely-sliced mushrooms and spring onions. Boil for 1 minute. Serve immediately.

Turkey Stock

Keep your turkey carcass to make a stock which may be used as the basis of a delicious soup or in St Stephen's Day Pie (see page 26).

1 turkey carcass
turkey giblets, i.e. heart, gizzard, neck
4.6–5.7 L (8–10 pints/20–25 cups) approx. water
2 onions, cut in quarters
2 leeks, split in two
2 sticks celery, cut in half
2 carrots, cut in half
a few parsley stalks
2 sprigs of thyme
6 peppercorns
no salt

Break up the carcass as much as possible. Put all the ingredients into a saucepan and cover with cold water. Bring to the boil and skim off any scum or fat. Simmer for 4–5 hours, then strain and remove any remaining fat. If you need a stronger flavour, boil down the liquid in an open pan to reduce by one-half the volume. *Do not* add salt.

Note: Stock will keep for several days in the fridge. If you want to keep it for longer, boil it up again for 5 or 6 minutes, allow it to get cold and refrigerate again or freeze.

If you have a ham bone, it could also be used in the stock for extra flavour.

White Winter Vegetable Soup
SERVES 8–9

55 g (2 ozs/½ stick) butter
110 g (4 ozs/1 cup) onions
140 g (5 ozs/1 cup) potatoes
140 g (5 ozs/1 cup) white turnips, cut into 5 mm (¼ inch) dice
110 g (4 ozs/1 cup) celery, cut into 5 mm (¼ inch) dice
110 g (4 ozs/1 cup) parsnips, cut into 5 mm (¼ inch) dice
110 g (4 ozs/1 cup) white part of leeks, cut into 5 mm (¼ inch) dice
140 g (5 ozs/1 cup) cauliflower, cut into 5 mm (¼ inch) dice
1.7 L (3 pints/7½ cups) home-made chicken stock
170–225 ml (6–8 fl ozs/¾–1 cup) creamy milk
salt and freshly-ground pepper

Garnish
finely-chopped chives
croûtons

Prepare all the vegetables. Melt the butter in a heavy saucepan; when it foams, add the potatoes and onions, and toss until well coated with butter. Cover with a paper lid (to keep in the steam) and the saucepan lid, sweat for 5 minutes approx. on a gentle heat, then add in the other diced vegetables. Season with salt and freshly-ground pepper, cover and sweat for a further 5 minutes. Discard the paper lid. Add the stock; bring it to the boil and simmer until the vegetables are soft, 8–10 minutes approx. Liquidise the soup, taste and thin with creamy milk if necessary.

Serve in soup bowls or in a soup tureen garnished with a blob of whipped cream, and sprinkle with a very few finely-chopped chives. Serve with croûtons on top.

Pink Grapefruit and Pomegranate Salad

SERVES 4–6

Pomegranates or wine apples have a short season — from November to the end of December or early January.

---

2 pink grapefruit
2 pomegranates
1–2 tablesp. (4–8 American teasp.) castor sugar

Garnish
mint *or* lemon balm leaves

Peel the skin from the grapefruit with a sharp knife so that all the pith is removed. You could use the skin to make Pamelas (see page 89).

Segment the grapefruit and put in a bowl.

Take one of the pomegranates and roll it backwards and forwards on the table to crush the seeds inside, then press the skin with the fingers. When the pomegranate feels quite soft inside, pierce a little hole in the side and squeeze out as much juice as possible into the bowl with the grapefruit. Cut the pomegranate in half and scoop out the seeds into a nylon sieve. Press any remaining juice out of the seeds over the grapefruit.

Cut the other pomegranate in half and carefully remove the seeds, clearing them of all the white pith. Put the seeds into the bowl with the grapefruit.

Sprinkle with sugar and taste for sweetness. Leave to macerate for at least an hour.

Serve chilled in pretty white bowls or on plates. Garnish with mint or lemon balm leaves.

Grape and Melon with Mint
SERVES 5–6

The honeydew melon — which is the one most widely available around Christmas — is not the most flavourful of the melon family, however this recipe turns it into a delicious starter. The flavour of Grape and Melon with Mint is immeasurably better if the grapes are peeled and pipped.

225 g (8 ozs/2 cups) green grapes
1 small *or* ½ large melon (check first that it is fully ripe)
2 oranges (not too large)
1 lemon
1 tablesp. (4 American teasp.) approx. castor sugar
1 teasp. finely-chopped fresh mint

Garnish
5–6 tiny sprigs of fresh mint

Cut the ripe melon in half; discard the seeds and scoop the flesh into balls with a melon-baller if you have one. Alternatively, cut it neatly into 1 cm (½ inch) dice. (Scrape the fleshy bits off the skin so that there is no waste, and hide them in the bottom of the bowl under the melon balls: they will still taste delicious!)

Squeeze the juice from the oranges and lemon, pour it over the melon and stir in the sugar. Peel the whole grapes and remove the pips with the hooked end of a sterilised paper clip or hair grip. (There is no quick way to do this: the best thing is to make yourself a cup of coffee, sit up on a high stool and listen to something riveting on the radio!)

Stir the peeled and pipped grapes into the melon, with a little freshly-chopped mint if you have it. Taste and add a little more sugar if necessary. Cover the bowl with cling-film and chill until ready to serve.

Serve in pretty white bowls. Garnish each one with a sprig of fresh mint.

Salad of Smoked Salmon and Avocado

SERVES 4

110–170 g (4–6 ozs) smoked Irish salmon
1 avocado
¼ cucumber
salt and freshly-ground pepper
sugar
a few drops of wine vinegar
a little chopped fennel
a mixture of salad leaves, e.g. frisée, butterhead, rocket, golden marjoram, salad burnet, some herb flowers

Dressing
1 tablesp. (4 American teasp.) wine vinegar
3 tablesp. (4 American tablesp.) olive oil
salt and freshly-ground pepper

Garnish
sprigs of fennel

Whisk the oil and vinegar together, season with salt and freshly-ground pepper. Wash and dry the lettuces (if they are too large, tear them gently into bite-sized pieces). Put into a bowl and cover with cling-film until needed.

To assemble the salad: Dice the cucumber and sprinkle with salt, pepper, sugar and a few drops of wine vinegar. Halve the avocado and cut it into a fan shape; place one-quarter of the avocado on each plate. Brush with olive oil. Sprinkle the cucumber with chopped fennel. Cut the smoked salmon into thin slices and arrange beside the avocado, perhaps in a rose shape.

Toss the salad leaves in the dressing. Arrange between the avocado and salmon, and sprinkle cucumber dice over the salad. Garnish with tiny sprigs of fennel and serve immediately.

Rosette of Smoked Salmon with Cucumber and Dill
SERVES 4

This is a very stylish way to serve a little smoked salmon with a cucumber salad.

170–225 g (6–8 ozs) piece of smoked salmon (allow 45 g (1½ ozs) approx. per person)
½ cucumber, sliced very thinly
salt and freshly-ground pepper
sugar
¼ teasp. finely-chopped dill *or* ½ teasp. fennel
1 tablesp. wine vinegar

Garnish
flat parsley, dill, fennel *or* chervil leaves

Mix the thinly-sliced cucumber with the vinegar and season with salt, freshly-ground pepper and enough sugar to get a sweet-sour salad. Sprinkle with dill or fennel and leave to macerate for at least 30 minutes.

Cut the smoked salmon in thin slices straight down onto the skin, and arrange the slices to form a rosette in the centre of 4 white plates. Arrange the cucumber slices in a circle around the smoked salmon, and grind a little pepper over the smoked salmon.

Garnish with dill, flat parsley or chervil. Serve with fresh brown bread and butter, and offer segments of lemon separately.

Oyster au Nature
SERVES 2 FOR A FEAST!

Native Irish oysters are in season from September to March, when there's an 'r' in the month! They are known to be an aphrodisiac — worse than standing under the mistletoe — so beware!

2 dozen native Irish oysters

Garnish
seaweed
1 lemon
a little crushed ice

Oysters must be tightly shut: if a shell is even *slightly* open, discard it.

Not long before serving, open the oysters. You will need an oyster knife for this operation. Place the oyster on the worktop, deep shell down. Cover your hand with a folded tea-towel and hold the oyster firmly. Put the tip of the oyster knife into the crevice at the hinge of the oyster, push hard and then quickly twist the knife. You need to exert quite a bit of pressure (hence it is essential that the hand holding the oyster is protected, in case the knife slips!). When you feel the oyster is opening, change the angle of the knife and, keeping the blade close to the shell, slice the oyster off the top shell in one movement. Then run the knife underneath the oyster in the deep shell and flip it over: be careful not to lose any of the delicious juices.

Put a bed of seaweed on 2 chilled plates, place the oysters on the seaweed and add a few segments of lemon.

Serve with fresh brown soda bread and butter and perhaps a glass of stout.

Smooth Turkey Liver Pâté
SERVES 10–12

225 g (8 ozs) fresh turkey livers *or* turkey and chicken livers, minced
(1 turkey liver weighs 110–140 g (4–5 ozs), depending on the size of
the bird. Make up the balance with chicken livers.)
30 ml (2 tablesp./⅛ cup) brandy *or* medium sherry
225–340 g (8–12 ozs/2–3 sticks) butter (depending on how strong the livers
are)
1 teasp. fresh thyme leaves
1 large clove of garlic, made into a paste
salt and freshly-ground pepper
clarified butter to seal the top

Wash the livers and remove any membrane or green tinged bits. Melt a little butter in a frying pan; when the butter foams, add in the livers and cook over a gentle heat. Be careful not to overcook them or the outsides will get crusty: all traces of pink should be gone. Put the livers through a sieve or into a food processor. De-glaze the pan with brandy or sherry, allow to flame, add the garlic and then scrape out the pan with a spatula and add to the livers. Allow to cool, then add the butter and fresh thyme leaves and process for 1 minute or until absolutely smooth. Season carefully, taste and add more butter if necessary.

Fill the Pâté into individual ramekins or one large pottery bowl. Decorate with some fresh thyme leaves and seal with clarified butter. Refrigerate to set the top butter.

Serve with hot crusty bread or toast.

Clarified butter:
Melt 225 g (8 oz/2 sticks) butter gently in a saucepan or in the oven. Allow it to stand for a few minutes, then spoon the crusty white layer of salt particles off the top of the melted butter. Underneath this crust there is clear liquid butter which is called clarified butter. The milky liquid at the bottom can be discarded or used in a béchamel sauce.

Clarified butter is excellent for cooking because it can withstand a higher temperature when the salt and milk particles are removed. Clarified butter will keep covered in a fridge for several weeks.

Main Courses

Here you will find many favourite Christmas recipes — Traditional Roast Turkey with Fresh Herb Stuffing, Glazed Ham or Bacon, and Old-fashioned Roast Goose with Potato and Apple Stuffing. Many readers may be disappointed to discover that I am including only one recipe for Roast Stuffed Turkey, no exciting-sounding recipes full of chestnuts, sausage meat and walnuts; the answer is that I feel there's nothing to beat a really good old-fashioned roast turkey with a buttery fresh herb stuffing and I have never yet tasted an alternative stuffing that I enjoyed, so I'm not going to dream one up just for the sake of excitement! Order your turkey in plenty of time from a reputable poulterer or supplier. For best flavour choose a free-range bird with a good plump breast and unblemished skin. Obviously it depends on the size of the family but a medium sized turkey of 4.5–5.4 kg (10–12 lbs) is easiest to cook in most domestic ovens and doesn't dry out.

People ask me over and over again what to do with left-over turkey and I say, tongue in cheek, buy a smaller turkey so you don't have so much left over. I cannot understand why people insist, year in year out, in buying turkeys that are much too large for their particular situation; and then by the time it is eaten they are so fed up of left-over turkey that they don't want to see it again for another year!

Why not be sensible this year and buy a bird which will just about feed the family with perhaps a little left over for a pie on St Stephen's Day, or a few sandwiches. The carcass may then be boiled up for stock to make a delicious light turkey broth. Keep the liver for a pâté which will keep in your fridge for several days and be a great stand-by for snacks or a starter at a moment's notice.

Turkey with Ham and Mushrooms à la Crème is a simply delicious recipe for people who want to have a really carefree Christmas Day; it takes a good deal of advance preparation but the whole meal, turkey, ham and potato may be frozen and reheated with delicious results. Christmas wouldn't be the same without Spiced Beef; again properly-made spiced beef will keep for weeks, basically because most spices have strong antiseptic qualities. Serve it with Chutney, or Cumberland Sauce, slices of avocado and perhaps a cucumber salad and a Winter Green Salad.

14

Traditional Roast Goose with Potato Stuffing is impossible for me to resist.
Geese are always free-range and usually rather more expensive than turkey.
Geese are of a tremendously independent nature and simply will not thrive if
they are confined for too long. When I was younger, from time to time I
entertained all sorts of romantic notions about being a real farmer's wife.
Once I thought I would rear some geese for Christmas and of course it was
disastrous because I couldn't bear to kill them, so they roamed freely around
and became very cheeky, tyrannical and arrogant and finally chased our
guests away — strong men who would brave any watch dog would take to
their heels if attacked by a goose or, even more amusingly, refuse to budge
from the car. What became of the geese? Well, I gave them away for presents
— live! The Potato Stuffing for the Roast Goose is also delectable and would
be equally good with a plump free-range duck.

If there are just two of you, Roast Pheasant makes a perfect Christmas
dinner; treat yourself to all the trimmings, crispy Game Chips, Cranberry
Sauce and maybe a Bread Sauce too as an extra treat. One can't help feeling
proud when taking a beautifully glazed ham out of the oven, delicious either
hot or cold and it will be a tremendous stand-by for several meals.

For some reason we tend to think of meat dishes at Christmas, so after
Christmas I often long for fish. Monkfish with Mushrooms and Herbs is a
wonderful recipe because it can be made ahead and reheated if necessary
and is perfect for large parties, either as a starter or main course. Pipe a ruff
of mashed potato around the edge and you have the whole meal in one dish.

Old-fashioned Roast Turkey with Fresh Herb Stuffing and Bread Sauce
SERVES 10–12

This is my favourite roast stuffed turkey recipe. You may think the stuffing
seems dull because it doesn't include exotic-sounding ingredients like
chestnuts and spiced sausage meat, but in fact it is moist and full of the
flavour of the herbs and the turkey juices. Cook a chicken in exactly the
same way but use one-quarter of the stuffing quantity given.

1 x 4.5–5.4 kg (10–12 lbs) free-range turkey with neck and giblets

Fresh herb stuffing
170 g (6 ozs/1½ sticks) butter
340 g (12 ozs/3 cups) chopped onions
400–450 g (14–16 ozs/7–8 cups) approx. soft breadcrumbs
8 tablesp. (2 ozs/1 cup) freshly-chopped herbs, e.g. parsley, thyme, chives, marjoram, savoury, lemon balm
salt and freshly-ground pepper

Stock
neck, gizzard, heart, wishbone and wingtips of turkey
2 sliced carrots
2 sliced onions
1 stick celery
bouquet garni
3 or 4 peppercorns

For basting the turkey
225 g (8 ozs/2 sticks) butter
large square of muslin (optional)

Garnish
large sprigs of fresh parsley *or* watercress

Remove the wishbone from the neck end of the turkey, for ease of carving later. Make a turkey stock by covering with cold water the neck, gizzard, heart, wishbone, wingtips, vegetables and bouquet garni. (Keep the liver for Smooth Turkey Liver Pâté, see page 11.) Bring to the boil and simmer while the turkey is being prepared and cooked, 3 hours approx.

To make the fresh herb stuffing: Sweat the onions gently in the butter until soft, for 10 minutes approx., then stir in the crumbs, herbs and a little salt and pepper to taste. Allow it to get quite cold. If necessary wash and dry the cavity of the bird, then season and half-fill with *cold* stuffing. Put the remainder of the stuffing into the crop at the neck end.

Weigh the turkey and calculate the cooking time. Allow 15 minutes approx. per 450 g (1 lb) and 15 minutes over. Melt 225 g (8 ozs/2 sticks) butter and soak a large piece of good-quality muslin in the melted butter; cover the turkey completely with the muslin and roast in a preheated moderate oven, 180°C/350°F/regulo 4, for 3–3½ hours. There is no need to baste it because of the butter-soaked muslin. The turkey browns beautifully, but if you would like it even browner, remove the muslin 10 minutes before the end of the cooking time.

Alternatively, smear well the breast, leg and crop with soft butter, and season with salt and freshly-ground pepper. If the turkey is not covered with butter-soaked muslin then it is a good idea to cover the whole dish with tin foil. However, your turkey will then be semi-steamed, not roasted in the traditional sense of the word.

The turkey is done when the juices run clear. To test, prick the thickest part at the base of the thigh and examine the juices: they should be clear. Remove the turkey to a carving dish, keep it warm and allow it to rest while you make the gravy.

To make the gravy: Spoon off the surplus fat from the roasting pan. De-glaze the pan juices with fat-free stock from the giblets and bones. Using a whisk, stir and scrape well to dissolve the caramelised meat juices from the roasting pan. Boil it up well, season and thicken with a little roux if you like. Taste and correct the seasoning. Serve in a hot gravy boat.

If possible, present the turkey on your largest serving disk, surrounded by golden crispy potatoes, and garnished with large sprigs of parsley or watercress and maybe a sprig of holly. Make sure no-one eats the berries!

Serve with Bread Sauce.

Bread Sauce
SERVES 12

I love Bread Sauce but if I hadn't been reared on it I might never have tried it — the recipe sounds so dull!

570 ml (1 pint/2½cups) milk
85–110 g (3–4 ozs/1½–2 cups) breadcrumbs
2 onions, each stuck with 6 cloves
55 g (2 ozs/½ stick) butter
salt and freshly-ground pepper
115–170 ml (4–6 fl ozs/½–¾ cup) thick cream

Bring to the boil in a small, deep saucepan all the ingredients except the cream. Season with salt and freshly-ground pepper. Cover and simmer gently on a very low heat or cook in a low oven, 160°C/325°F/regulo 3, for 30 minutes. Remove the onion and add the cream just before serving. Correct the seasoning and add a little more milk if the sauce is too thick.

Serve hot.

Clockwise from left

Rosette of Smoked Salmon with Cucumber and Dill; Grape and Melon with Mint presented in two different ways; Carrot and Parsnip Soup

Old-fashioned Roast Turkey with Fresh Herb Stuffing, Bread Sauce and Gravy; Roast Potatoes

St Stephen's Day Pie with Duchesse Potato

Apple, Celery and Walnut Salad

Baked Potatoes with Various Fillings

Traditional Roast Goose with Potato Stuffing and Apple Sauce
SERVES 8–10

Roast Goose with Potato Stuffing is almost my favourite winter meal. However, a word of warning! A goose looks enormous because it has a large carcass. Many people have been caught out by imagining that it will serve more people than it does. Allow 450 g (1 lb) cooked weight per person. This stuffing is also quite delicious with duck but use one-quarter of the quantity given below.

1 x 4.5 kg (10 lbs) approx. goose

Stock
neck, giblets and wishbone of goose
1 sliced onion
1 sliced carrot

Bouquet garni
a sprig of thyme
3 or 4 parsley stalks
a stick of celery
6 or 7 peppercorns
cold water to cover

Stuffing
30 g (1 oz/¼ stick) butter
450 g (1 lb/4 cups) chopped onions
450 g (1 lb) cooking apples, e.g. Bramley Seedling, peeled and chopped
2–3 tablesp. (1 fl oz/scant ⅛ cup) fresh orange juice
900 g (2 lbs) potatoes
1 teasp. each thyme and lemon balm
¼ teasp. finely-grated orange rind
salt and freshly-ground pepper

To make the stuffing: Melt the butter in a heavy saucepan. Add the onions, cover and sweat on a gentle heat for about 5 minutes; add the apples, herbs and orange juice. Cook covered until the apples are soft and fluffy. Meanwhile, boil the potatoes in their jackets until cooked, peel, mash and add to the fruit and onion mixture. Add the orange rind and seasoning. Allow it to get quite cold before stuffing the goose.

To prepare the goose: Gut the goose and singe off the pin feathers and down if necessary. Remove the wishbone from the neck end. Combine the stock ingredients in a saucepan, cover with cold water and simmer for 1½–2 hours. Season the cavity of the goose with salt and freshly-ground pepper; rub a little salt into the skin also. Stuff the goose loosely and roast for 2 hours approx. in a preheated moderate oven, 180°C/350°F/regulo 4.

Prick the thigh at the thickest part; the juices which run out should be clear. If they are still pink, the goose needs a little longer. When cooked, remove the goose to a serving dish and put it in a very low oven while you make the gravy.

To make the gravy: Spoon off the surplus fat from the roasting tin (save for sautéeing or roasting potatoes — it keeps for months in a fridge). Add about 570 ml (1 pint) of the strained giblet stock to the roasting tin and bring to the boil. Using a small whisk, scrape the tin well to dissolve the meaty deposits which are full of flavour. Taste for seasoning and thicken with a little roux if you like a thickened gravy. If the gravy is too weak, boil it for a few minutes to concentrate the flavour; if it's too strong, add a little water or stock. Strain and serve in a hot gravy boat.

Carve the goose and serve the Apple Sauce and gravy separately.

Apple Sauce
SERVES 8

The trick with Apple Sauce is to cook it on a very low heat with only a tiny drop of water so that it is nice and thick and not too watery.

450 g (1 lb) cooking apples (Bramley Seedling *or* Grenadier)
1–2 dessertsp. (2–4 American teasp.) water
55 g (2 ozs/¼ cup) approx. sugar (depending on how tart the apples are)

Peel, quarter and core the apples; cut the pieces in two and put them in a stainless steel or cast-iron saucepan, with sugar and water. Cover and cook on a very low heat until the apples break down in a fluff. Stir and taste for sweetness.

Serve warm or cold.

Roast Pheasant or Guinea Fowl with Game Chips and Cranberry Sauce

SERVES 2–3

A Roast Pheasant makes the perfect Christmas dinner for two and you'll probably have a little left over which may be eaten cold for supper. This slightly unorthodox way of cooking the pheasant produces a moist, juicy bird. Guinea fowl is also wonderful cooked and served in this way.

1 young, plump pheasant or guinea fowl
45 g (1½ ozs/scant ½ stick) butter
85 g (3 ozs/¾ cup) chopped onions
70 g (2½ ozs/1¼ cups) breadcrumbs
1 tablesp. (4 American teasp.) freshly-chopped herbs, e.g. parsley, thyme, chives, marjoram
salt and freshly-ground pepper

Gravy
285 ml (½ pint/1¼ cups) game *or* chicken stock

1 x blue 'J' cloth (don't use a pink one or the dye will run and you will have an extraordinary-looking bird!)
55 g (2 ozs/½ stick) butter

Gut the pheasant if necessary and remove the 'crop' which is at the neck end; wash and dry well.

To make the stuffing: Melt the butter and sweat the onions until soft but not coloured, then remove from the heat. Stir in the soft white breadcrumbs and herbs, season with salt and freshly-ground pepper and taste. Unless you are about to cook the bird right away, allow the stuffing to get quite cold before putting it into the bird.

Season the cavity with salt and freshly-ground pepper and stuff the pheasant loosely. Sprinkle the breast also with salt and freshly-ground pepper. Melt the butter and soak the 'J' cloth in it. Wrap the pheasant completely in the 'J' cloth (fear not, the 'J' cloth will not melt: you can even wash it out and use it later!).

Roast in a preheated moderate oven, 190°C/375°F/regulo 5, for 1¼ hours approx. Test by pricking the leg at the thickest point: the juices should just run clear. Remove the 'J' cloth from the pheasant and keep warm on a serving dish while you make the gravy.

Spoon off any surplus fat from the roasting pan (keep it for roasting or sautéeing potatoes). De-glaze the pan with game or chicken stock. Bring it to the boil, and use a whisk to dislodge the crusty caramelised juices so they can dissolve into the gravy. Season with salt and freshly-ground pepper, taste and boil until you are happy with the flavour. Pour into a hot gravy boat.

Carve the pheasant and serve with stuffing, gravy, Game Chips and Cranberry Sauce — a simply delicious Christmas dinner for two!

Game Chips

SERVES 4

Game Chips are traditionally served with roast pheasant but they are also very good with guinea fowl or just as a snack with a drink.

450 g (1 lb) large, even-sized potatoes
olive oil for deep frying
salt

Wash and peel the potatoes. For even-sized chips, trim each potato with a swivel-top peeler until smooth. Slice them very finely, preferably on a mandolin. Soak in cold water to remove the excess starch (this will also prevent them from discolouring or sticking together). Drain off the water and dry well.

Heat the olive oil to 180°C/350°F/regulo 4. Drop in the dry potato slices a few at a time and fry until golden and completely crisp. Drain on kitchen paper and sprinkle lightly with salt. Repeat until they are all cooked.

If they are not to be served immediately, they may be stored in a tin box and reheated in a low oven just before serving.

Cranberry Sauce

SERVES 6 APPROX.

Cranberry Sauce is also delicious served with roast turkey, game and some rough pâtés and terrines.

170 g (6 ozs/1½ cups) fresh cranberries
60 ml (4 tablesp./¼ cup) water
85 g (3 ozs/scant ½ cup) granulated sugar

Put the fresh cranberries in a heavy-based stainless steel or cast-iron saucepan with the water — don't add the sugar yet as it tends to toughen the skins. Bring them to the boil, cover and simmer until the cranberries 'pop' and soften, about 7 minutes. Remove from the heat and stir in the sugar until dissolved.

Serve warm or cold.

Note: Cranberry Sauce will keep in your fridge for a week to 10 days.

Glazed Ham with Cumberland Sauce
SERVES 12–15

A perfectly-glazed ham always looks stunning but loin of bacon is ideal for this recipe also and is much easier to carve.

1 x 4.5–5.4 kg (10–12 lbs) fresh *or* slightly smoked ham (make sure it has a nice layer of fat)
1 small tin of pineapple (use about 85–115 ml (3–4 fl ozs/½ cup) of the juice)
340–450 g (12 ozs–1 lb/1½–2 cups) brown demerara sugar
60–80 whole cloves, depending on the size of the diamonds

If the ham is salty, soak it in cold water overnight; next day discard the water. Cover the ham with fresh cold water and bring it slowly to the boil. If the meat is still salty there will be a white froth on top of the water. If this is the case it is preferable to discard this water, cover the ham with fresh cold water again and repeat the process. Finally, cover the ham with hot water and simmer until it is almost cooked. Allow 20 minutes to 450 g (1 lb) approx. for ham, 15 minutes for a loin of bacon.

Peel off the rind, cut the fat into a diamond pattern and stud each diamond with a whole clove. Blend the brown sugar to a paste with a *little* pineapple juice. Be careful not to make it too liquid. Spread this over the ham. Bake it in a hot oven, 250°C/500°F/regulo 9, for 20 minutes or until the top has caramelised. While it is glazing, baste regularly with the syrup and juices.

Serve hot or cold with Cumberland Sauce.

Cumberland Sauce

SERVES 8–12 APPROX.

Serve with cold ham, turkey, chicken, guinea fowl, game or rough pâtés.

1 orange
1 lemon
225 g (8 ozs/¾ cup) red currant jelly
55 ml (3–4 tablesp./¼ cup) port
a pinch of cayenne pepper
a pinch of ground ginger

With a swivel-top peeler, remove the peel very thinly from the orange and half of the lemon (make sure there is no white pith). Shred into thin julienne strips, cover with cold water, bring to the boil and simmer for 4–5 minutes. Strain off the water and discard it, then refresh the peel under cold water. Strain and keep it aside.

Squeeze the juice from the fruit and put it into a stainless steel saucepan with the jelly and spices; allow it to melt down. Then add the peel and port to the sauce. Boil it rapidly for 5–10 minutes.

Test like jam by putting a little blob on a cold saucer. When it cools it should wrinkle slightly.

Cumberland Sauce may be served in a bowl right away or it may be potted up and kept until needed, like jam.

Ballymaloe Spiced Beef with Spiced Tomato Sauce

SERVES 12–16

Although Spiced Beef is traditionally associated with Christmas, in Cork we eat it all year round! It may be served hot or cold and is a marvellous stand-by, because if it is properly spiced and cooked it will keep for 3–4 weeks in a fridge.

1.35–1.8 kg (3–4 lbs) lean flap of beef *or* silverside
Ballymaloe spice for beef

This delicious recipe for Spiced Beef has been handed down in Myrtle Allen's family and is the best I know. It includes saltpetre, nowadays regarded as a health hazard, so perhaps you should not live exclusively on it! Certainly people have lived on occasional meals of meats preserved in this way, for generations.

The recipe below makes enough spice to cure 5 flanks of beef, each 1.8 kg (4 lbs) approx. in size.

Ballymaloe Spice for Beef

225 g (8 ozs/1¼ cups) demerara sugar
340 g (12 ozs/1¼ cup) salt
15 g (½ oz/2 American teasp.) saltpetre (available from chemists)
85 g (3 ozs/generous ½ cup) whole black pepper
85 g (3 ozs/generous 1 cup) whole allspice (Pimento *or* Jamaican pepper)
85 g (3 ozs/1 cup) whole juniper berries

Grind all the ingredients (preferably in a food processor) until fairly fine. Store in a screw-top jar; it will keep for months, so make the full quantity even if it is more than you need at a particular time.

To prepare the beef: If you are using flank of beef, remove the bones and trim away any unnecessary fat. Rub the spice well over the beef and into every crevice. Put into an earthenware dish and leave in a fridge or cold larder for 3–7 days, turning occasionally. (This is a dry spice, but after a day or two some liquid will come out of the meat.) The longer the meat is left in the spice, the longer it will last and the more spicy the flavour.

Just before cooking, roll and tie the joint neatly with cotton string into a compact shape, cover with cold water and simmer for 2–3 hours or until soft and cooked. If it is not to be eaten hot, press by putting it on a flat tin or into an appropriate sized bread tin; cover it with a board and weight and leave for 12 hours.

Spiced Beef will keep for 3–4 weeks in a fridge.

To serve, cut it into thin slices and serve with some freshly-made salads and home-made chutneys, or in sandwiches.

Spiced Tomato Sauce
MAKES 900 G (2 LBS) APPROX. SAUCE

900 g (2 lbs) very ripe tomatoes, preferably cherry tomatoes
140 g (5 ozs/1¼ cups) sliced onions
285 g (10 ozs/1¼ cups) sugar
2 teasp. salt
1 level teasp. allspice
285 ml (½ pint/1¼ cups) red wine
285 ml (½ pint/1¼ cups) white wine vinegar
1 teasp. mashed green peppercorns

Put the tomatoes into a deep bowl and cover with boiling water. Leave for 1 minute approx. Pour off the water then slash the skin and squeeze out the tomatoes. The fruit should pop out leaving the empty skin in your fingers. In order to keep a good red colour, boil the tomatoes with all the ingredients, except the green peppercorns, in a wide shallow stainless steel pan for rapid evaporation. When reduced to about one-half, add the peppercorns and cook for another 5 minutes. It should be quite thick. Pot into jam jars and cover as for jam. The sauce should keep for 6 months or more. Serve with cheese or cold meats.

Note: White wine and red vinegar may be used instead of red wine and white vinegar.

Turkey with Ham and Mushrooms à la Crème
SERVES 30 APPROX.

This recipe is just the answer to everyone's prayers at Christmas. The whole Christmas dinner in a dish with piped potato all around the edge, it can even be cooked a week ahead and frozen. Although it makes enough for about 30 people which is ideal for a party, you can prepare it in 2, 3 or 4 large dishes and if necessary freeze it and use just 1 dish at a time.

1 x 5.4–6.3 kg (12–14 lbs) free-range turkey
1 x 3.6–4.5 kg (8–10 lbs) ham (unsmoked, soaked overnight in cold water if salty)
chicken *or* turkey stock
dry white wine
2 carrots
1 large sliced onion
2 sticks of celery
bouquet garni
a few peppercorns
3 tablesp. (1½ ozs/⅓ cup) chopped parsley
2 tablesp. (¼ cup) other fresh herbs, e.g. tarragon, thyme, chives, lemon balm
3–4 egg yolks
570 ml (1 pint/2½ cups) cream
85 g (3 ozs) roux
Duchesse Potato made with 5.4–6.3 kg (12–14 lbs) potato, for piping around the dishes

Mushrooms à la Crème

1.125 kg (2½ lbs) sliced mushrooms
340 ml (12 fl ozs/1½ cups) cream
2½ tablesp. (⅓ cup) fresh herbs, e.g. parsley, thyme, chives
425 g (15 ozs/3¾ cups) onions, finely chopped
85–110 g (3–4 ozs/¾–1 stick) butter
lemon juice
salt and freshly-ground pepper

Cover the ham with cold water, bring it slowly to the boil and discard the water; cover again with cold water. If a lot of white scum floats to the top, throw out this water also, otherwise continue to simmer until the ham is cooked, 2½ hours approx. (calculate 20 minutes to 450 g (1 lb) as a rough guide). The skin will peel off easily when the ham is cooked.

Meanwhile, season the turkey and put it into a large saucepan with about 12.5–15 cm (5–6 inches) of water or chicken stock and white wine. Add 1 large sliced onion, 2 sticks of celery, a bouquet garni and a few peppercorns. Bring to the boil, cover closely and simmer for 2 hours approx. either on the top of the stove or in a moderate oven, 180°C/350°F/regulo 4.

While the turkey and ham are cooking, prepare the Mushrooms à la Crème. Melt the butter in a wide, heavy-bottomed saucepan. Add the onions, cover and sweat over a low heat until soft. Remove and keep aside. Fry the mushrooms, a few at a time, just covering the bottom of the pan. Season with salt and freshly-ground pepper. Take them off as soon as they go limp and add them to the onions. Add more butter if necessary, but never too much. When cooked, put the lot back into the saucepan, add the herbs, cream and a squeeze of lemon juice. Taste for seasoning. Thicken with about 85 g (3 ozs) roux. Set the Mushrooms à la Crème aside until ready to assemble the dish.

When the turkey is cooked, remove it from the casserole and de-grease the cooking liquid. Bring it to the boil and reduce by half; add 285–425 ml (½–¾ pint/1¼–1⅞ cups) of cream and thicken to a light coating consistency with roux. Taste for seasoning. Chop up the brown turkey meat and the white meat from the wings into smallish pieces and mix with the Mushrooms à la Crème. Add 2 tablesp. (8 American teasp.) chopped parsley, 1 dessertsp. (2 American teasp.) thyme, chives and lemon balm if available.

Spread a layer of the sauce on the serving dishes, carve a nice slice of ham for each serving and place at regular intervals on top of the sauce. Spoon some of the brown meat and mushrooms mixture on top. Carve the turkey breast into thin slices and place 1 slice per serving on top of the mushrooms and ham.

Mix 3–4 egg yolks with 140 ml (¼ pint/⅔ cup) cream to make a liaison, blend well and stir this into the rest of the sauce. (It should be a coating consistency.) Coat the pieces of turkey with this sauce.

Pipe a generous border of Duchesse Potato (see page 38) all around the edge of the dishes. Cool the dishes quickly, cover and refrigerate or freeze until needed. Reheat in a moderate oven, 180°–190°C/350°–375°F/regulo 4–5, for 30 minutes approx. until it is bubbling and golden brown on top. If necessary, flash under a grill to brown the edges of the Duchesse Potato.

Garnish with sprigs of fresh parsley and serve.

St Stephen's Day Pie

SERVES 12

Try to keep some left-over turkey and ham for this delicious pie — it's the most scrumptious way to use up left-overs and can be topped with fluffy mashed potatoes or a puff pastry lid.

900 g (2 lbs) cold turkey meat
450 g (1 lb) cold ham *or* bacon
30 g (1 oz/¼ stick) butter
340 g (12 ozs/3 cups) chopped onions
1 clove of garlic
855 ml (1½ pint/3⅔ cups) well-flavoured Turkey Stock (see page 6) *or* 570 ml (1 pint/2½ cups) stock and 285 ml (½ pint/1¼ cups) turkey gravy
225 g (8 ozs) flat mushrooms *or* button if flats are not available
1 tablesp. (4 American teasp.) chopped parsley
1 tablesp. (4 American teasp.) chopped chives
2 teasp. fresh marjoram *or* tarragon if available
140 ml (¼ pint/⅔ cup) cream
450 g (1 lb) puff *or* flaky pastry *or* 900 g (2 lbs) Duchesse Potato (see page 38)

2 x 1.1 L (2 pints/5 cups) capacity pie dishes

Cut the turkey and ham into 2.5 cm (1 inch) approx. pieces. Melt the butter in a heavy saucepan, add the chopped onions, cover and sweat for about 10 minutes until they are soft but not coloured. Meanwhile wash and slice the mushrooms. When the onions are soft, stir in the garlic and remove to a plate. Increase the heat and cook the sliced mushrooms, a few at a time. Season with salt and freshly-ground pepper and add to the onions and garlic. Toss the cold turkey and ham in the hot saucepan, using a little extra butter if necessary; add to the mushrooms and onion. De-glaze the saucepan with the turkey stock. Add the cream and chopped herbs. Bring it to the boil, thicken with roux, add the meat, mushrooms and onions and simmer for 5 minutes. Taste and correct the seasoning.

Fill into the pie dishes, and pipe rosettes of potato all over the top. Bake in a moderate oven, 190°C/375°F/regulo 5, for 15–20 minutes or until the potato is golden and the pie is bubbling.

Alternatively, if you would like to have a pastry crust, allow the filling to get quite cold. Roll out the pastry to about 3 mm (⅛ inch) thickness, then cut a strip from around the edge the same width as the lip of the pie dish. Brush the edge of the dish with water and press the strip of pastry firmly down onto it; wet the top of the strip again. Cut the pastry into an oval just slightly larger than the pie dish. Press this down onto the wet border, flute the edge of the pastry with a knife and then scallop them at 2.5 cm (1 inch) approx. intervals. Roll out the trimmings and cut into leaves to decorate the top. Make a hole in the centre to allow the steam to escape while cooking.

Brush with egg wash and bake in a preheated hot oven, 250°C/475°F/regulo 9, for 10 minutes; then turn the heat down to moderate, 180°C/350°F/regulo 4, for 20–25 minutes or until the pastry is cooked through and the pie is bubbling.

Serve with a green salad.

Monkfish with Mushrooms and Herbs
SERVES 8

Scallops and several other kinds of firm-textured fish can be used in this delicious creamy fish dish. It is perfect to make in large quantities because it can be cooked ahead and reheated later.

1.125 kg (2½ lbs) monkfish tails, well trimmed and cut into collops (1 cm (½ inch) thick slices, cut at an angle)
85 g (3 ozs/¾ cups) finely-chopped onions
30 g (1 oz/¼ stick) butter
85 g (3 ozs/¾ cup) flour
dry white wine
fish stock (see recipe below)
225 g (8 ozs/2½ cups) sliced mushrooms
1–2 tablesp. freshly chopped parsley, thyme and fennel, mixed
salt and freshly-ground pepper
creamy milk
110 g (4 ozs/1 cup) grated cheddar cheese (optional)
Duchesse Potato for piping around the serving dish (optional) (see page 38)

Put the collops of monkfish into a stainless steel or cast-iron saucepan, cover with half wine and half fish stock or water. Bring to the boil and poach gently for 3–4 minutes and remove fish as soon as it is cooked (it will lose its opaque look and be white the whole way through). Reduce the cooking liquid to 340 ml (12 fl ozs/1½ cups) approx.

Meanwhile, sweat the onions in melted butter for 5–8 minutes, add the sliced mushrooms, season with salt and freshly-ground pepper and cook for 3–4 minutes more. Stir in the flour and cook for about 1 minute. Bring the fish cooking liquid up to 700 ml (1¼ pints/generous 3 cups) by adding creamy milk. Stir it into the onion and mushrooms and bring to the boil. Add the freshly-chopped herbs, taste and reduce until the flavour is strong enough. Correct the seasoning, add the monkfish and about half the cheese to the sauce and simmer for 2–3 minutes.

Pipe a border of Duchesse Potato around the serving dish, spoon the monkfish and sauce into the centre, sprinkle with the remaining cheese and reheat, or cool and reheat later. This takes about 25–30 minutes in a moderate oven, 190°C/375°F/regulo 5.

Serve with a good green salad.

Fish Stock

Fish stock takes only 20 minutes to make. If you can get lots of nice fresh fish-bones from your fishmonger it's well worth making 2 or 3 times this stock recipe, because it freezes perfectly and then you will have fish stock at the ready for any recipe.

15 g (½ oz/⅛ stick) butter
100 g (3½ ozs/scant 1 cup) onions
1.010 kg (2¼ lbs) fish-bones, preferably sole, turbot *or* brill
115 ml (4 fl ozs/½ cup) dry white wine
cold water to cover the bones
4 peppercorns
bouquet garni containing a sprig of thyme, 4–5 parsley stalks, small piece of celery and a tiny scrap of bay-leaf

Chop the fish-bones into pieces and wash thoroughly under cold running water until no trace of blood remains. Slice the onions finely. In a large stainless steel saucepan melt the butter, add the onions and sweat them on a gentle heat until soft but not coloured. Add the bones to the saucepan, stir and cook very briefly with the onions. Add the dry white wine and boil until nearly all the wine has evaporated. Add cold water, peppercorns and a large bouquet garni. Bring to the boil and skim; simmer for 20 minutes, skimming often. Strain.

Vegetables

My husband Tim who is a vegetable and fruit grower, holds very strong views on how vegetables should be treated. His view is (and I very much sympathise with it) that if cooks and chefs properly understood all the months of tender loving care that go into producing perfect vegetables, they might treat them with more care and hover over the saucepan to catch them just at the right moment.

I love winter vegetables, so hearty and comforting, yet many of them are considered to be poor relations of summer vegetables. Jerusalem artichokes, parsnips, sprouts, leeks, red cabbage, celery and the humble swede turnip, all delicious; why do we so seldom see these vegetables on restaurant menus, just the endless imported French beans, sugar peas and tiny tasteless premature carrots?

The current trend towards 'pre-washed' vegetables is, in my view, a move very much in the wrong direction. I know it's much more convenient to buy vegetables pre-washed, but there is no comparison in flavour. Have we really got to the stage where we can't manage to scrub a few carrots or spuds ourselves? For the few minutes it takes, it's well worth it, for the sake of better flavour and better nutrients and vitamins for our families. Also, unwashed vegetables when you can get them are cheaper and they keep for longer.

Potatoes are very important to Irish people, most of us eat them once if not twice a day. They are a wonderfully nutritious food particularly if cooked with their skins on. Do you know why the Cork people are so 'frightfully superior' to everyone else? Well I'll let you into a secret. It's because they 'ates them skin and all' and that gives them the edge over everyone else, so there you are now!

But even though we all love our spuds there has been much criticism of both the flavour and keeping quality over the past few years and in some city areas sales of potatoes have actually gone down, people have got so weary of bad quality. Part of the reason for the drop in quality is that Irish potato growers must compete with much cheaper imports. Ireland does not have an ideal climate for potato growing; we're very prone to blight and only certain varieties are suitable for our moist damp conditions. They happen to be the varieties that have excellent flavour but unfortunately produce lowish yields. In order to compete with the cheaper imports, many Irish potato growers decided to boost their yields by putting more nitrogen onto their crops and so the potatoes grew bigger and more watery and of course didn't keep well either. Consumers very soon started to grumble, potato sales went down, and the poor growers found themselves in a 'catch 22' situation yet again. But sadly for the consumer the simple fact of the matter is that if we want really good quality Irish potatoes that haven't been boosted with too much nitrogen, we'll have to pay more.

I would also like to see a situation where potatoes are not just called Irish potatoes but are also labelled with the name of the particular grower, so that if one finds particularly good potatoes she can identify them again the next time she goes shopping or avoid them as the case may be. However, things are improving; many growers have realised the problem and have taken measures to remedy the situation.

I would also like to see the actual variety marked on home-produced vegetables in shops, so that the interested shopper may be aware of the tremendous variation in flavour between different varieties.

Brussels Sprouts
SERVES 4–6

The traditional way to cook Brussels sprouts was to cut a cross in the stalk so that they would, hopefully, cook more evenly. However, I discovered that if you cut them in half they cook much faster and taste much more delicious.

---

450 g (1 lb) Brussels sprouts cut lengthways top to bottom
30–55 g (1–2 ozs/¼–½ stick) butter
salt and freshly-ground pepper

Choose even, medium-sized sprouts. Trim the outer leaves if necessary and cut in half. Bring 570 ml (1 pint) water to a fast rolling boil and add 1½ teaspoons of salt. Toss in the sprouts, keep the lid off the saucepan and boil furiously for 5 or 6 minutes or until the sprouts are cooked through but still have a slight bite. Pour off the water.

Melt a little butter in the bottom of a saucepan, roll the sprouts gently in the butter and season with lots of freshly-ground pepper and salt. Taste and serve immediately in a hot serving dish.

Note: If the Brussels sprouts are not to be served immediately, it is best to refresh them under cold water just as soon as they are cooked. Then, just before serving, drop them into boiling salted water for a few seconds to heat through. Drain and toss in butter, season and serve. This way they will taste almost as good as if they were freshly cooked — much more delicious than sprouts that keep warm for half an hour in an oven or a hostess trolley.

Braised Celery
SERVES 4–6

1 head of celery
30–55 g (1–2 ozs/¼–½ stick) butter
1 tablesp. (4 teasp.) olive oil
salt and freshly-ground pepper

Garnish
freshly-chopped parsley

Pull the stalks off the head of celery. If the outer stalks seem a bit tough, peel the strings off with a swivel-top peeler or else use these tougher stalks in the stockpot. Cut the stalks into 1 cm (½ inch) chunks.

Melt the butter and the olive oil in a cast-iron casserole, toss in the celery and stir until well coated. Season with salt and freshly-ground pepper. Cover and cook on a gentle heat for 15–20 minutes approx. Add a few spoons of poultry, beef or game gravy if you have it, and cook for a few minutes uncovered.

Serve in a hot dish, sprinkled with some freshly-chopped parsley.

Red Cabbage
SERVES 6–8

450 g (1 lb) red cabbage (Red Drummond)
450 g (1 lb) cooking apples (Bramley Seedling)
1 tablesp. (4 American teasp.) wine vinegar
1 heaped tablesp. approx. sugar
1 level teasp. salt
115 ml (4 fl ozs /½ cup) water

Remove any damaged outer leaves from the cabbage. Examine and clean it if necessary. Cut in quarters, remove the core and slice the cabbage finely across the grain. Put the vinegar, water, salt and sugar into a cast-iron casserole or stainless steel saucepan. Add the cabbage and bring it to the boil. Meanwhile, peel and core the apples, cut into quarters (no smaller). When they are ready, lay them on top of the cabbage, cover and continue to cook gently until the cabbage is tender, about 30–50 minutes. Do not overcook or the colour and flavour will be ruined. Taste for seasoning and add more sugar if necessary.

Serve in a warm serving dish.

Note: Some varieties of red cabbage are quite tough and don't seem to soften much, even with prolonged cooking. Our favourite variety, Red Drummond, gives best results.

Braised Jerusalem Artichokes
SERVES 4

Jerusalem artichokes are a perennial winter vegetable; once you plant them, they usually re-emerge every year and even spread if you are not careful. The flavour is particularly good with game, beef or shellfish.

675 g (1½ lbs) Jerusalem artichokes
30 g (1 oz /¼ stick) butter
1 dessertsp. (2 American teasp.) water
salt and freshly-ground pepper
chopped parsley

Peel the artichokes thickly and slice 5 mm (¼ inch) thick. Melt the butter in a cast-iron casserole, toss the artichokes and season with salt and freshly-ground pepper. Add water and cover with a paper lid (to keep in the steam) and the saucepan lid. Cook on a low heat or put in a moderate oven, 180°C/350°F/regulo 4, until the artichokes are soft but still keep their shape, 15–20 minutes approx. (Toss every now and then during cooking.)

Serve sprinkled with chopped parsley.

Clockwise from left

Traditional Sherry Trifle; Plum Pudding; Christmas Bombe

Preparation of Chocolate Caraque

Croque au Chocolat with Tangerine Mousse and Chocolate Craqué

Bread and Butter Pudding

Iced Chocolate Oranges

Marzipan Apples

Buttered Leeks
SERVES 4–6

Many people dislike leeks, I think possibly because they have only had them boiled. Try them this way — they are meltingly tender and mild in flavour.

4 medium-sized leeks
45 g (1½ ozs/generous ¼ stick) butter
1 dessertsp. (2 American teasp.) water if necessary
salt and freshly-ground pepper
chopped parsley *or* chervil

Cut off the dark green leaves from the top of the leeks (wash and add these to the stock pot or use for making green leek soup). Slit the leeks lengthwise about half way down the centre and wash well under cold running water. Slice into 5 mm (¼ inch) rounds.

Melt the butter in a heavy saucepan; when it foams, add the sliced leeks and toss gently to coat with butter. Add the water. Season with salt and freshly-ground pepper. Cover with a paper lid (to keep in the steam) and a close-fitting lid. Reduce the heat and cook very gently for 20–30 minutes approx., or until soft and moist. Check and stir every now and then.

Serve in a warm serving dish, sprinkled with chopped parsley.

Note: The pot of leeks may be cooked in the oven if that is more convenient, 150°C/300°F/regulo 2, for about the same length of time.

Swede Turnip
SERVES 6 APPROX.

Swede turnips are looked upon as a very mundane vegetable, but a really good purée with lots of butter and pepper and salt is one of the tastiest winter vegetables, particularly good with ham or bacon.

900 g (2 lbs) swede turnips
salt and lots of freshly-ground pepper
55–110 g (2–4 ozs/½–1 stick) butter

Garnish
1 tablesp. (4 American teasp.) finely-chopped parsley

Peel the turnip and cut into 2 cm (¾ inch) approx. cubes. Cover with water (ham or bacon cooking water would be delicious). Add a good pinch of salt, bring to the boil and simmer until soft. Strain off the water, mash the turnip well and beat in the butter. Taste and season with lots of pepper and more salt if necessary.

Roast Parsnips

SERVES 6–8

3 parsnips
beef dripping *or* olive oil

Peel the parsnips, cut them into quarters and leave them that size unless they are very large. Blanch them in boiling water for 4–5 minutes depending on size. Drain, then refresh them under cold water, and dry. Put them around a roast so that they will become soft and golden brown in the juices and fat of the meat. Alternatively, you could roast parsnips in a separate pan with beef dripping or olive oil in a hot oven, 230°C/450°F/regulo 8. They could roast in the same pan as potatoes. Cooked this way they will be crisper outside; turn them frequently so that they do not become too crusty.

Buttered Parsnips

SERVES 4

675 g (1½ lbs) parsnips
salt and freshly-ground pepper
chopped parsley
55–85 g (2–3 ozs/½–¾ stick) butter

Peel the parsnips thinly. Cut off the tops and tails and cut them into wedges. Remove the inner core if it seems to be at all woody; divide the wedges into 2 cm (¾ inch) approx. cubes. Blanch them in boiling salted water for 2–3 minutes. Drain and refresh with cold water.

Melt the butter in a casserole and toss the parsnips until they are coated; season with salt and plenty of pepper. Cover and keep them over a low heat to finish cooking, turning carefully from time to time. They should look golden and be slightly soft but not mushy. Taste and add more seasoning if necessary.

Sprinkle with parsley and serve right away.

Baked Potatoes with Various Fillings
SERVES 8–16

8 x 225 g (8 ozs) unpeeled 'old potatoes', e.g. Golden Wonders *or* Kerrs
Pinks
1 egg
70 g (2½ ozs/generous ½ stick) butter
45–85 ml (1½–3 fl ozs/3–6 tablesp.) milk
salt and freshly-ground pepper

Scrub the skins of the potatoes very well. Prick each potato 3 or 4 times and
bake in a preheated hot oven, 200°C/400°F/regulo 6, for 1 hour approx.,
depending on size. When cooked, cut the potatoes in half lengthways, scoop
out the centre and mash carefully. Mix with some milk and butter. Season
with salt and freshly-ground pepper.

Cheese and Onion Filling

4–8 spring onions, depending on size (there should be 1 dessertsp. approx.
for each potato)
55 g (2 ozs/½ stick) butter
110 g (4 ozs/1 cup) grated cheddar cheese
1 tablesp. (4 American teasp.) chopped parsley

Sweat the chopped onion in butter until soft. Add the mashed potato,
chopped parsley and half the cheese; taste and season if necessary. Fill back
into the potato skins. Sprinkle with the remaining cheese and put back into
an oven, if still hot, or under a grill until golden and bubbling on top.

Mushroom and Bacon Filling

6 tablesp. (1 cup) Mushrooms à la Crème (see page 25)
4–6 rashers, green *or* smoked bacon *or* dice of left-over ham *or* bacon
1 tablesp. (4 American teasp.) chopped parsley
a little creamy milk

Fry the rashers until crisp. Cut them into small strips, stir into the
Mushrooms à la Crème and add parsley. Half fill the potato skins with the
potato mixture. Spoon some mushroom and bacon on top. Add a little
creamy milk to make the remaining potato softer and then pipe it around the
edge to form a border. Reheat in a moderate oven or under the grill.

Other Suggestions

1. Smoked mackerel with Mushrooms à la Crème
2. Smoked haddock with cheese and béchamel (white sauce)
3. Peeled tomatoes softened in butter with scallions, topped with béchamel sauce and sprinkled with cheese
4. Blue cheese and bacon
5. Mushrooms à la Crème with left-over bits of turkey and ham

Roast Potatoes

Everybody loves roast potatoes, yet people ask me over and over again for the secret of golden crispy roast potatoes.

1. Well, first and foremost buy good quality 'old' potatoes, e.g. Golden Wonders, Kerrs Pinks, Pennella, or British Queens. New potatoes are not suitable for roasting.
2. Peel them just before roasting.
3. Do not leave them soaking in water or they will be soggy inside because of the water they absorb. This always applies, no matter how you cook potatoes. Unfortunately, many people have got into the habit of peeling and soaking potatoes even if they are just going to boil and mash them.
4. Dry potatoes carefully, otherwise they will stick to the tin, and when you turn them over you will lose the crispy bit underneath.
5. If you have a fan oven it is necessary to blanch and refresh the potatoes first, then proceed as below.
6. Heat the olive oil or fat in the roasting pan and toss the potatoes to make sure they are well coated in the olive oil or fat.
7. Roast in a hot oven, 230°C/450°F/regulo 8, basting occasionally, for 30–60 minutes, depending on size.
8. For perfection, potatoes should be similar in size and shape.

Champ

SERVES 4–6

This is one of the most delicious Irish potato recipes. A bowl of champ flecked with green scallions is 'comfort' food at its best!

6–8 unpeeled 'old' potatoes, e.g. Golden Wonders *or* Kerrs Pinks
110 g (4 ozs/1 cup) chopped scallions *or* spring onions (use the bulb and green stem) *or* 45 g (1½ ozs/½ cup) chopped chives
340 ml (12 fl ozs/1½ cups) milk
55–110 g (2–4 ozs/½–1 stick) approx. butter
salt and freshly-ground pepper

Scrub the potatoes and boil them in their jackets. Chop finely the scallions or spring onions or chives. Cover with cold milk and bring slowly to the boil. Simmer for about 3–4 minutes, turn off the heat and leave to infuse. Peel and mash the freshly-boiled potatoes and, while hot, mix with the boiling mix and onions; beat in the butter. Season to taste with salt and freshly-ground pepper.

Serve in 1 large or 6 individual bowls with a knob of butter melting in the centre.

Champ may be put aside and reheated later in a moderate oven, 180°C/350°F/regulo 4. Cover with tin foil while it reheats so that it doesn't get a skin.

Potato Cakes

Serves 8

Left-over mashed or Duchesse Potato may be used for potato cakes. They are delicious even with just a few crispy rashers.

900 g (2 lbs) unpeeled 'old' potatoes, e.g. Golden Wonders or Kerrs Pinks
2 tablesp. flour
1–2 eggs
30–55 g (1–2 ozs/¼–½ stick) butter
creamy milk
1 tablesp. chopped parsley, chives and lemon thyme, mixed
seasoned flour
salt and freshly-ground pepper
bacon fat, butter or olive oil for frying

Cook the potatoes in their jackets, pull off the peel and mash right away; add the beaten eggs, butter, flour and herbs. Season with lots of salt and freshly-ground pepper, adding a few drops of creamy milk if the mixture is altogether too stiff. Taste and correct the seasoning. Shape into potato cakes about 7.5 cm (3 inches) diameter and scant 2.5 cm (1 inch) thick. Dip in seasoned flour.

Melt some bacon fat, butter or olive oil in a frying pan on a gentle heat. Fry the potato cakes until golden on one side, then flip over and cook on the other side, 4–5 minutes approx. each side; they should be crusty and golden.

Serve on hot plates with a blob of butter melting on top.

Duchesse Potato or Fluffy Mash

SERVES 4

900 g (2 lb) unpeeled potatoes, preferably Golden Wonders *or* Kerrs Pinks
285 ml (½ pint/10 fl ozs) creamy milk
1–2 egg yolks *or* 1 whole egg and 1 egg yolk
30–55 g (1–2 ozs/¼–½ stick) butter

Scrub the potatoes well. Put them into a saucepan of cold water, add a good pinch of salt and bring to the boil. When the potatoes are about half cooked, 15 minutes approx. for 'old' potatoes, strain off two-thirds of the water, replace the lid on the saucepan, put onto a gentle heat and allow the potatoes to steam until they are cooked.

Peel immediately by just pulling off the skins, so you have as little waste as possible, mash while hot (see below). (If you have a large quantity, put the potatoes into the bowl of a food mixer and beat with the spade.)

While the potatoes are being peeled, bring about 285 ml (½ pint) of milk to the boil. Beat the eggs into the hot mashed potatoes, and add enough boiling creamy milk to mix to a soft light consistency suitable for piping; then beat in the butter, the amount depending on how rich you like your potatoes. Taste and season with salt and freshly-ground pepper.

Note: If the potatoes are not peeled and mashed while hot and if the boiling milk is not added immediately, the Duchesse Potato will be lumpy and gluey.

If you only have egg whites they will be fine and will make a delicious light mashed potato also.

Apple, Celery and Walnut Salad

SERVES 6

This salad — similar to the Waldorf Salad invented by the chef of the Waldorf Astoria in New York — is delicious with cold meats, particularly ham. The tart combination of apple and celery makes it an excellent counterbalance to rich meats such as duck or pork, or it may be served as a first course on its own.

225 g (8 ozs) green dessert apples
225 g (8 ozs) red dessert apples
2 tablesp. (8 American teasp.) lemon juice
1 level teasp. castor sugar
140 ml (¼ pint/generous ½ cup) mayonnaise
½ head of celery
55 g (2 ozs/½ cup) shelled fresh walnuts
1 crisp lettuce

Garnish
sprigs of watercress
freshly-chopped parsley

Keep aside a half red and a half green apple. Wash and core the remainder, and cut into 1 cm (½ inch) dice. Make a dressing by mixing the lemon juice, castor sugar and 1 tablesp. (4 American teasp.) of mayonnaise. Toss the diced apple in the dressing and let it stand while you prepare the celery. Separate the celery, wash and chop or julienne the stalks into 4 cm (1½ inch) lengths. Put them into a bowl of iced water for 15–30 minutes. Chop the walnuts roughly. Add the celery and walnuts to the diced apple with the rest of the mayonnaise, and mix thoroughly. Slice the remaining red and green apples and sprinkle them with castor sugar and lemon juice.

Line a serving bowl with the clean crisp lettuce leaves and pile the salad into the centre. Arrange the apple slices around the bowl, alternating red and green.

Garnish with sprigs of watercress and some chopped parsley over the centre.

Note: To serve as a first course, arrange a few lettuce leaves on a white plate and pile a few tablespoons of salad into the centre. Arrange the slices of the red and green apple around the edge. Garnish with sprigs of watercress, sprinkle with parsley and serve.

Winter Green Salad with Herbed Vinaigrette Dressing

For this salad, use a selection of winter lettuces and salad leaves, e.g. butterhead, iceberg, raddichio, endive, chicory and sorrel. Tips of purple sprouting broccoli are also delicious and if you feel like something more robust, use some finely-shredded savoy cabbage and maybe a few shreds of red cabbage also.

First, make the dressing.

Herbed Vinaigrette Dressing

170 ml (6 fl ozs/¾ cup) extra virgin olive oil
80 ml (4 tablesp./⅜ cup) cider vinegar
1 teasp. Irish honey
1 clove of garlic, crushed
5 g (2 tablesp./¼ cup) freshly-chopped mixed herbs, e.g. parsley, chives, mint, watercress, thyme
salt and freshly-ground pepper

Put all the dressing ingredients into a screw-topped jar, adding salt and freshly-ground pepper to taste. Shake well to emulsify before use; otherwise, whiz together all the ingredients into a food processor or liquidiser for a few seconds. As a variation you could use 4 tablesp. (⅜ cup) of fresh lemon juice or wine vinegar instead of cider vinegar.

Wash and dry the lettuces and salad leaves and tear into bite-sized pieces. Put them into a deep salad bowl, add the sliced cabbage and toss it all together.

Just before serving, add a little dressing and toss until the leaves just glisten with dressing.

Desserts

You need to be in the full of your health to digest many of the traditional Christmas puddings, yet they are perennial favourites that have stood the test of time. This section includes both my mother's and my mother-in-law's favourite Plum Pudding recipes, one served with Brandy Butter and the other with a seriously fattening and totally irresistible sauce. Eat one on the first evening after they have been steamed for 5 hours, and keep the rest for Christmas — you might even like to eat the last one at Easter. If you can't be tempted in that direction how about the Christmas Bombe? This may be made well ahead of Christmas and whipped out of the freezer at a moment's notice — the Butterscotch Sauce keeps for weeks in a jar.

Also here are Mince Pies made with a very 'short' shortcrust pastry and Ballymaloe Home-Made Mincemeat (this mincemeat is the most delicious recipe I have tasted and it keeps for several years in a glass jar in a cold larder).

I've also included a 'proper' Trifle made with sweet sherry and a home-made sponge cake and an egg custard. (Sorry, no jelly or hundreds-and-thousands; trifle is probably the most abused recipe ever, but this one bears no resemblance to the travesty which is served up under the name of trifle in many establishments.)

Virtually all the puddings in this section may be prepared ahead with the possible exception of the Mince Pies, tarts and the Fresh Fruit Salad. The last, which takes only a few minutes to put together, is made from readily-available fruit and will be welcome after rich meals.

Croque au Chocolat with Tangerine Mousse and Iced Chocolate Oranges on the other hand, are what I call 'high stool jobs'. They certainly take some time and dedication but they may be done well in advance and the end result is guaranteed to produce gasps of admiration and lots and lots of well-deserved compliments. Don't forget to try the Marzipan Apples; for this recipe the apples are filled with marzipan and then rolled in cinnamon and castor sugar.

Last but not least you've got to try the Bread and Butter Pudding. I put it in on the pretext of using up left-over stale 'sliced pan' after Christmas, but when you taste it you won't need an excuse to make it next time. It also reheats really well even after a few days.

Mince Pies with Whiskey Cream

MAKES 20–24 MINCE PIES

450 g (1 lb) Ballymaloe Mincemeat (see page 82)

Pastry
225 g (8 ozs/2 cups) plain flour
110–170 g (4–6 ozs/1–1½ sticks) butter
a pinch of salt
1 dessertsp. (2 American teasp.) icing sugar
a little beaten egg *or* egg yolk and water to bind
egg wash

First make the pastry. Sieve the flour into a bowl; cut the butter into 1 cm
(½ inch) approx. cubes, toss into the flour and rub in with the finger tips.
Add the salt and the icing sugar. Mix with a fork as you gradually add in the
beaten egg (do this bit by bit because you may not need all the egg), then
use your hand to bring the pastry together into a ball: it should not be wet or
sticky. Cover with cling-film and refrigerate for an hour. Roll out the pastry
until quite thin, stamp out into rounds 7.5 cm (3 inches) diameter and line
shallow bun tins; put a good teaspoonful of mincemeat into each tin, damp
the edges with water and put another round on top. Egg wash and decorate
with pastry leaves, holly berries, etc.

Bake the mince pies in a preheated moderate oven, 180°C/350°F/regulo 4,
for 30 minutes approx. Allow them to cool slightly, then dredge with icing or
castor sugar.

Serve hot with whiskey-flavoured cream.

Whiskey Cream

225 ml (8 fl ozs/1 cup) whipped cream
1 teasp. icing sugar
1½–3 tablesp. (2–4 American tablesp.) Irish whiskey

Fold the sugar and whiskey into the cream.

Elizabeth O'Connell's Plum Pudding with Mrs Hanrahan's Sauce

It was always the tradition in our house to eat the first plum pudding on the
evening it was made. As children we could hardly contain ourselves with

excitement — somehow that plum pudding seemed all the more delicious because it was our first taste of Christmas. The plum pudding was usually made about mid November and everyone in the family had to stir so they could make a wish!

This recipe makes 2 large or 3 medium puddings. The large size will serve 10–12 people, the medium will serve 6–8.

340 g (12 ozs/2 cups) raisins
340 g (12 ozs/2 cups) sultanas
340 g (12 ozs/2 cups) currants
340 g (12 ozs/2¼ cups) brown sugar
340 g (12 ozs/6 cups) white breadcrumbs
340 g (12 ozs/3 cups) finely-chopped suet
110 g (4 ozs/½ cup) candied peel (preferably home-made)
2 cooking apples, diced *or* grated
rind of 1 lemon
3 pounded cloves (½ teasp.)
a pinch of salt
6 eggs
70 ml (2½ fl ozs/generous ¼ cup) Jamaica Rum
110 g (4 ozs/¾ cup) chopped almonds

Mix all the ingredients together very thoroughly and leave overnight; don't forget, everyone in the family must stir and make a wish! Next day stir again for good measure. Fill into pudding bowls; cover with a double thickness of greaseproof paper which has been pleated in the centre, and tie it tightly under the rim with cotton twine, making a twine handle also for ease of lifting.

Steam in a covered saucepan of boiling water for 6 hours. The water should come half way up the side of the bowl. Check every hour or so and top up with boiling water if necessary. After 6 hours, remove the pudding. Allow to get cold and re-cover with fresh greaseproof paper. Store in a cool dry place until required.

On Christmas Day or whenever you wish to serve the plum pudding, steam for a further 2 hours. Turn the plum pudding out of the bowl onto *a very hot serving plate*, pour over some whiskey or brandy and ignite. Serve immediately on *very hot plates* with Brandy Butter or Mrs Hanrahan's Plum Pudding Sauce.

You might like to decorate the plum pudding with a sprig of holly; however, take care, because the last time I did that I provided much merriment by setting the holly *and* my fringe on fire — as well as the pudding!

Mrs Hanrahan's Sauce

This recipe is so delicious that people ask to have more Plum Pudding just so that they can have an excuse to eat lots of sauce. This makes a large quantity but the base will keep for several weeks in the fridge, so you can use a little at a time, adding whipped cream to taste.

225 g (8 ozs/scant 1¼ cups) Barbados sugar (moist, soft, dark-brown sugar)
70 ml (2½ fl ozs/generous ¼ cup) port
70 ml (2½ fl ozs/generous ¼ cup) medium sherry
1.3–1.4 L (2¼–2½ pints/5⅝–6¼ cups) lightly-whipped cream
110 g (4 ozs/1 stick) butter
1 egg

Melt the butter, stir in the sugar and allow it to cool slightly. Whisk the egg, and add to the butter and sugar with the sherry and port. Refrigerate.

When needed, add the lightly-whipped cream to taste.

This sauce is also very good with mince pies and other tarts.

Myrtle Allen's Plum Pudding with Brandy Butter
Serves 8–10

Making the Christmas Puddings
(from *The Ballymaloe Cook Book* by Myrtle Allen)
The tradition that every member of the household could have a wish which was likely (note, never a firm promise) to come true, was, of course, a ruse to get all the children to help with the heavy work of stirring the pudding. I only discovered this after I was married and had to do the job myself. This recipe, multiplied many times, was made all at once. In a machineless age, mixing all those expensive ingredients properly was a formidable task. Our puddings were mixed in an enormous china crock which held the bread for the household for the rest of the year. My mother, nanny and the cook took it in turns to stir, falling back with much panting and laughing after a few minutes' work. I don't think I was really much help to them.

Christmas puddings should be given at least 6 weeks to mature. They will keep for a year. They become richer and firmer with age, but one loses the lightness of the fruit flavour. We always eat our last plum pudding at Easter.

If possible, prepare your own fresh beef suet — it is better than the pre-packed product.

170 g (6 ozs/1 cup) shredded beef suet
170 g (6 ozs/¾ cup) sugar
200 g (7 ozs/4 cups) soft breadcrumbs
225 g (8 ozs/1½ cups) currants
225 g (8 ozs/1½ cups) raisins
110 g (4 ozs/¾ cup) candied peel
1–2 teasp. mixed spice
a pinch of salt
2 tablesp. (8 teasp.) flour
55 ml (2 fl ozs/¼ cup) flesh of a baked apple
3 eggs
55 ml (2 fl ozs/¼ cup) Irish whiskey

1 x 1.7 L (3 pints/7½ cups) capacity pudding bowl

Mix the dry ingredients thoroughly. Whisk the eggs and add them, with the apple and whiskey. Stir very well indeed. Fill into the greased pudding bowl. Cover with a round of greaseproof paper or a butter-wrapper pressed down on top of the pudding. Put a large round of greaseproof or brown paper over the top of the bowl, tying it firmly under the rim.

Place in a saucepan one-third full of boiling water and simmer for 10 hours. Do not allow the water to boil over the top and do not let it boil dry either. Store in a cool place until needed.

Boil for 1½–2 hours before serving. Left-over pudding may be fried in butter.

Serve with Whiskey Cream or Brandy Butter.

Brandy Butter

85 g (3 ozs/¾ stick) butter
85 g (3 ozs/⅜ cup) icing sugar
2–6 tablesp. brandy

Cream the butter until very light, add the icing sugar and beat again. Then beat in the brandy, drop by drop. If you have a food processor, use it: you will get a wonderfully light and fluffy Brandy Butter.

Traditional Sherry Trifle
SERVES 8–10

Sherry Trifle, the pudding to be avoided at all costs on most restaurant menus, can be a revelation when it's made as it should be, with good home-made ingredients and lots of best-quality sweet sherry.

450 g (1 lb) approx. home-made Sponge Cake *or* Swiss Roll
570 ml (1 pint/2½ cups) Light Pastry Cream (see page 48)
225 g (8 ozs/¾ cup) home-made raspberry jam (*Simply Delicious*, page 76)
140–170 ml (5–6 fl ozs/¾ cup) sweet *or* medium sherry

Garnish
570 ml (1 pint/2½ cups) whipped cream
8 cherries *or* crystallised violets
8 diamonds of angelica

1 x 1.7 L (3 pints/7½ cups) capacity glass bowl

Sandwich the rounds of Sponge Cake with raspberry jam in the usual way, or spread the Swiss Roll with jam and roll up lengthways. Make the Pastry Cream. Cut the Sponge or Swiss Roll into 2 cm (¾ inch) slices and line the glass bowl, sprinkling with sherry as you go along. Pour in some Pastry Cream and then add more of the Sponge or Swiss Roll. Sprinkle with the remainder of the sherry. Spread the Pastry Cream over the top. Cover with cling-film and leave for 5 or 6 hours, or preferably overnight, to mature.

Before serving, spread whipped cream over the top, pipe rosettes if you like and decorate with cherries or crystallised violets and diamonds of angelica.

Sponge Cake
SERVES 8

5 eggs
140 g (5 ozs/generous ½ cup) castor sugar
140 g (5 ozs/1 cup) flour

Filling
⅓ of a pot approx. home-made raspberry jam
castor sugar for sprinkling on top

2 x 23 cm (9 inches) tins

Grease the tins carefully with melted butter, dust with flour, cut out a circle of greaseproof paper and fit it neatly onto the base of each tin.

Put the eggs and sugar into a bowl and whisk until it is a pale and fluffy mousse. When you lift the whisk, make a figure of 8 on top: it should hold its shape for several seconds. Put the flour into a sieve and sift about one-third gently over the mousse; fold in the flour with a spatula or a long-handled metal spoon (*not* a wooden spoon) and then sieve in some more; repeat until all the flour is lightly folded in. Turn gently into the prepared tins and bake in a preheated oven, 190°C/375°F/regulo 5, for 20 minutes approx., until cooked. Turn out on a wire tray, peel off the greaseproof paper and allow to cool.

This sponge would also be delicious filled with fresh fruit and cream.

Swiss Roll

SERVES 8

---

110 g (4 ozs/¾ cup) plain flour
4 eggs
110 g (4 ozs/½ cup) castor sugar
2 tablesp. (8 American teasp.) warm water
½ teasp. vanilla essence
6 tablesp. (1 cup) warmed home-made raspberry jam (*Simply Delicious*, page 76)

---

1 x 25.5 cm (10 inches) x 38 cm (15 inches) Swiss roll tin

Preheat the oven to 190°C/375°F/regulo 5.

Line a large Swiss roll tin with greaseproof paper cut to fit the bottom of the tin exactly. Brush the paper and sides of the tin with melted butter, dust with flour and castor sugar.

Sieve the flour. Put the eggs and castor sugar into a bowl over a saucepan of simmering water. Whisk the mixture until it is light and fluffy. Take it off the heat and continue to whisk until the mixture is cool again. (If using an electric mixer, no heat is required.) Add the water and vanilla essence. Sieve in about one-third of the flour at a time and fold it into the mousse using a large metal spoon.

Pour the mixture gently into the tin. Bake in the preheated oven for 12–15 minutes. It is cooked when it feels firm to the touch in the centre. The edges will have shrunk in slightly from the sides of the tin. Lay a piece of greaseproof paper on the work top and sprinkle it evenly with castor sugar. Turn the Swiss roll tin onto the sugared greaseproof paper. Remove the tin and greaseproof paper from the bottom of the cake. While the cake is still warm, spread it sparingly with home-made raspberry jam. Catch the edge of the paper nearest you and roll up the Swiss Roll away from you.

Suggestions for other fillings: If you are not using the Swiss Roll as a basis for Trifle there are many other fillings you might like to try, but roll the greaseproof paper into the Swiss Roll while warm and unroll it later when cold to fill if you are using whipped cream.

1. Mashed banana with lemon juice and whipped cream
2. Melted chocolate and whipped cream
3. Fresh strawberries or raspberries mashed with a little sugar and whipped cream
4. Other home-made jam and whipped cream.

Light Pastry Cream

MAKES 570 ML (1 PINT) APPROX.

285 ml (½ pint/1¼ cups) milk
a vanilla pod *or* ½ teasp. pure vanilla essence
3 small eggs
110 g (4 ozs/½ cup) castor sugar
30 g (1 oz/scant ¼ cup) flour

In a heavy-bottomed saucepan, bring the milk just to the boil, with a small piece of vanilla pod in it, or add a few drops of vanilla essence afterwards. Separate the yolks and whites of 2 eggs. Whisk the yolks and the remaining whole egg with the sugar until light in colour. *Stir* in the flour then pour on the milk. Return all to the saucepan and stir over a gentle heat until it comes to the boil. Allow *actually to boil* for 2 minutes, still stirring all the time. (I find a little wire whisk better than a wooden spoon for this operation.) Stir with the whisk until the Pastry Cream is thick. Transfer to a bowl. Whisk the egg white stiffly in a clean bowl and fold into the Pastry Cream while still warm. Allow it to cool before using.

Iced Chocolate Oranges

SERVES 24 IF 2 SEGMENTS ARE SERVED PER PERSON
SERVES 12 IF 4 SEGMENTS ARE SERVED PER PERSON

Making these delectable Iced Chocolate Oranges will keep you out of mischief for several hours, however the end result is a very sophisticated dessert which keeps perfectly in a freezer for several weeks.

12 oranges

For ice-cream
225 ml (8 fl ozs/1 cup) water
4 tablesp. (⅓ cup) sugar
4 egg yolks

a simply delicious christmas

1.1 L (2 pints/5 cups) *whipped* cream
55 g (2 ozs) dark chocolate
30 g (1 oz) unsweetened chocolate
rind of 2 oranges

Garnish
tiny bay-leaves
1 orange
orange-flavoured cream

Cut the tops off the oranges, and scoop out the pulp carefully with a
teaspoon, keeping the 'shells' intact. Retain the tops to use as covers later.
Put the orange 'shells' into the freezer. Liquidise and sieve the pulp and
keep for Home-made Orange and Lemonade (see page 74). Put the sugar
and water into a saucepan, stir until all the sugar is dissolved, then bring
back to the boil. Continue to boil until the syrup reaches the thread stage.
It will look thick and syrupy; when a metal spoon is dipped in, the last drops
of syrup will form a thin thread. Pour this boiling syrup immediately onto the
whisked-up egg yolks and continue to whisk until it becomes a white, creamy
mousse. Divide this mousse into two bowls.

Melt the chocolate very carefully and add to one bowl; stir in half the softly-
whipped cream. Use to half-fill the orange 'shells'. Freeze (if you sit the
oranges into bun trays they will stay upright).

Grate the rind of 2 oranges and stir into the other half of the mousse and
fold in the remaining whipped cream. Fill up the orange 'shells' with the
orange ice-cream. Cover with the tops and return to the freezer — you will
probably have some orange ice-cream left over, so freeze separately.

To serve: When completely frozen, cut into quarters lengthways and arrange
on a white serving plate. Decorate with little rosettes of Orange-flavoured
Cream, little segments of orange and tiny bay-leaves.

Orange-flavoured Cream

225 ml (8 fl ozs/1 cup) whipped cream
grated rind of 1 orange
½–1 tablesp. (2–4 American teasp.) icing sugar

Mix the finely-grated orange rind into the cream and sweeten to taste with
icing sugar.

Croque au Chocolat with Tangerine Mousse and Chocolate Craqué

S~ERVES~ 12, ~MAKES~ 24 ~APPROX.~

These very stylish chocolate cases filled with Tangerine Mousse are a little fiddly to make but the end result is certainly well worth the effort.

Chocolate Cases
450 g (1 lb) best-quality dark chocolate
48 paper bun cases (use 2 papers for each chocolate case to give extra strength to the sides)

Melt the chocolate until smooth in a very low oven or in a bowl over hot water. Spread the chocolate evenly over the paper cases with the back of a teaspoon. Check that there are no 'see-through' patches when you hold them up to the light (it is a good idea to do a few extra cases to allow for accidents!).

Tangerine Mousse
2 eggs and 1 egg yolk
55 g (2 ozs/¼ cup) castor sugar
3 tangerines
1 heaped teasp. (2 American teasp.) gelatine
juice of 1 lemon
2 tablesp. (8 American teasp.) whipped cream

Garnish
2 tangerines
200 ml (7 fl ozs/⅞ cup) cream
castor sugar to taste
granted tangerine rind

Grate the tangerine rind on the finest part of a stainless steel grater. Put it into a bowl with the castor sugar, eggs and egg yolk. Whisk to a very thick mousse with an electric whisk (or put the bowl over a saucepan of hot water if a small quantity is made).

'Sponge' the gelatine in half the lemon juice, and then dissolve the granules by putting the bowl containing the gelatine and lemon juice into a saucepan of simmering water. Squeeze the tangerines, add the remainder of the lemon juice and make the juice up to 115 ml (4 fl ozs/½ cup) with water if necessary. Blend carefully with the gelatine mixture — add the juice into the gelatine to avoid strings — and then stir this mixture into the mousse. Cool, stirring occasionally, or put it over ice to speed it up. Fold in the softly-whipped cream just before it sets. Carefully peel the paper off the chocolate cases. Fill the cases two-thirds full with the mousse. Cover and chill until the mousse is completely set.

Meanwhile, fold the finely-grated tangerine rind into the cream and sweeten to taste with icing sugar. Just before serving, lay a thin slice of peeled tangerine on top. Decorate with tiny rosettes of flavoured cream and for a really stunning result add little pieces of Chocolate Craqué!

Chocolate Craqué

110 g (4 ozs) dark chocolate

Melt the chocolate and spread it thinly with a palette knife onto a marble slab. Allow it to set almost completely and then with a sharp knife or a paint scraper shave off long, thin scrolls. Use a slightly sawing movement and keep your hand upright. This is fun to do but there's quite a lot of skill involved — you'll get good at it with practice and you can always eat the rejects!

Christmas Bombe with Butterscotch Sauce
SERVES 12–16

This scrumptious Christmas Bombe is made up layers of three home-made ice-creams — chocolate, coffee and praline. It may be made several weeks ahead and is perfect for those who dislike Christmas Pudding.

1 x stainless steel *or* enamel pudding bowl, 2.3 L (4 pints/10 cups) capacity

Chocolate Ice-cream
110 g (4 tablesp./½ cup) sugar
225 ml (8 fl ozs/1 cup) water
4 egg yolks
1 teasp. vanilla essence
1.1 L (2 pints/5 cups) whipped cream
110 g (4 ozs/4 squares) plain chocolate
55 g (2 ozs/2 squares) unsweetened chocolate

Coffee Ice-cream
55 g (2 tablesp./¼ cup) sugar
115 ml (4 fl ozs/½ cup) water
2 egg yolks
½ teasp. boiling water
3 teasp. instant coffee
570 ml (1 pint/2½ cups) whipped cream

Praline Ice-cream
55 g (2 tablesp./¼ cup) sugar
115 ml (4 fl ozs/½ cup) water
2 egg yolks
½ teasp. pure vanilla essence
570 ml (1 pint/2½ cups) whipped cream
2 heaped tablesp. (8 American teasp.) praline

Praline
55 g (2 ozs/scant ½ cup) unskinned almonds
55 g (2 ozs/¼ cup) sugar

Garnish
285 ml (½ pint/1¼ cups) whipped cream

First make the chocolate ice-cream. Put the sugar and water into a saucepan, stir until all the sugar is dissolved, then bring back to the boil. Continue to boil until the syrup reaches the thread stage, 106°C–113°C/223°–236°F. It will look thick and syrupy; when a metal spoon is dipped in, the last drops of syrup will form a thin thread. Meanwhile, whisk the egg yolks until white and fluffy. When the syrup is at the correct stage, pour the boiling syrup gradually onto the egg yolks, whisking all the time. Continue to whisk until the mixture is a thick white mousse. Melt the two kinds of chocolate in a bowl over simmering water or in a very low oven. Cool it slightly. Add some of the mousse to the chocolate and stir quickly, add more and then mix the two mixtures together thoroughly; fold in the softly-whipped cream. Put the pudding bowl into the freezer for about 10 minutes, so that it will be icy cold. Line the bowl with the chocolate ice-cream in an even layer, put it into the freezer and after about 1 hour take it out and improve the shape if necessary.

Meanwhile make the praline and coffee ice-cream. First make the praline and set it aside. Put the unpeeled almonds and sugar in a small heavy-bottomed saucepan over a low heat. Do not stir until the sugar caramelises, then rotate the pan until all the nuts are coated with caramel. Turn onto an oiled tray and when the praline is cold and hard, crush it to a coarse powder.

Make the praline ice-cream as in the previous recipe to the mousse stage, then stir in the pure vanilla essence and fold in the cream. Put the ice-cream into a flat dish and freeze for about 1 hour, or until semi-frozen; then stir in the 2 heaped tablespoons of crushed praline powder. Wrap the pudding charms or 6 coins in greaseproof paper, push them into the side of the bombe, then make an even layer of praline ice-cream in the bowl. Leave the centre free to fill with coffee ice-cream.

While the bombe is freezing, make the coffee ice-cream. Again proceed as for the chocolate ice-cream to the mousse stage. Dissolve the instant coffee to a paste in ½ teaspoon of *boiling water*, mix some of the mousse into the coffee and then mix with the rest of the mousse; fold in the soft-whipped cream. Fill the coffee ice-cream into the centre of the bombe, cover the bowl with a plastic clip-on lid or cling-film and freeze solid. Leave overnight to set if possible.

To serve: Unmould the bombe and decorate with rosettes of whipped cream and crystallised violets and angelica or a sprig of holly. Serve with Butterscotch Sauce and scatter a little of the remaining praline over each helping.

Butterscotch Sauce

SERVES 12 APPROX.

This delicious sauce can be served with any ice-cream.

110 g (4 ozs/1 stick) butter
170 g (6 ozs/¾ cup) Barbados sugar (moist, soft, dark-brown sugar)
110 g (4 ozs/generous ½ cup) granulated sugar
285 g (10 ozs/¾ cup) golden syrup
225 ml (8 fl ozs/1 cup) cream
½ teasp. pure vanilla essence

Put the butter, sugars and golden syrup into a heavy-bottomed saucepan and melt gently on a low heat. Simmer for about 5 minutes, remove from the heat and gradually stir in the cream and the vanilla essence. Put back on the heat and stir for 2 or 3 minutes until the sauce is absolutely smooth.

Serve hot or cold.

Note: This sauce will keep for several weeks stored in a screw-top jar in the fridge.

Caramelised Cranberry Tart
Serves 8–10

1 x 24 cm (9½ inch) sweet shortcrust pastry tart shell, baked blind

Filling
285 ml (½ pint/1¼ cups) heavy whipping cream
285 g (10 ozs/1⅓ cups) granulated sugar
70 ml (2½ fl ozs/⅓ cup) water
285 g (10 ozs/2 cups) cranberries
2 large eggs, lightly whisked
½ teasp. finely chopped orange zest

Preheat the oven to 160°C/325°F/regulo 3.

Put the cream into a small saucepan and scald over a medium-high heat. Remove the cream from the heat and cover. Set aside.

Put the sugar and water in a saucepan. Stir over a medium heat until the sugar is dissolved. Increase the heat to high and cook the sugar until it is chestnut in colour. (Do not stir after you increase the heat.) Remove the saucepan from the stove and slowly add the cranberries, stirring until they release their juice and wilt slightly. Slowly add the warm cream, stirring constantly. Add the remaining cranberries. Cool for 4 or 5 minutes and gently whisk in the egg and orange zest.

Pour the mixture into the par-baked pie shell. Bake until thick, golden and bubbly, about 1 hour. Cool the tart on a wire rack before cutting. Serve with softly whipped cream.

Apple and Mincemeat Tart
Serves 8–12

The pastry in this recipe is particularly good and easy to make and may be used for many other tarts as well.

340 g (12 ozs/2 cups) flour
225 g (8 ozs/2 sticks) butter
2 eggs
55 g (2 ozs/scant ¼ cup) castor sugar
egg wash

Filling

3 or 4 cooking apples, e.g. Bramley Seedling

a little sugar if the apples are very tart

225 g (8 ozs/1 cup) Ballymaloe Mincemeat (see page 82)

1 x tin, 18 cm (7 inches) x 30.5 cm (12 inches) x 2.5 cm (1 inch) deep

Preheat the oven to 180°C/350°F/regulo 4.

Cream the butter and sugar together either by hand or in a food mixer. Add the eggs and beat for several minutes. Reduce speed and mix in the flour. This pastry needs to be chilled for at least 1 hour otherwise it is difficult to handle. (Better still, make it the day before you need it and chill it overnight.)

To make the tart: Roll out the pastry 3 mm (⅛ inch) approx. thick. Use slightly more than half to line the tin. Spread the mincemeat on the base of the tart. Peel, quarter and slice the apples into the mincemeat and sprinkle with sugar. Cover with a lid of pastry, seal the edges, decorate with pastry holly leaves and brush with egg wash. Bake in a preheated moderate oven, 180°C/350°F/regulo 4, until the apples are tender, 45 minutes–1 hour approx.

When cooked, cut into squares, sprinkle lightly with castor sugar and serve with softly-whipped cream.

Marzipan Apples

SERVES 12, 1 PER PERSON

A Swedish friend called Bo Hermansson gave me this mouth-watering recipe for baked apples. The centre is filled with home-made marzipan and then the apples are rolled in cinnamon-flavoured sugar.

12 medium eating apples, e.g. Worcester Pearmain, Golden Delicious *or* Cox's Orange Pippin

Marzipan

170 g (6 ozs/scant 2 cups) ground almonds

225 g (8 ozs/1 cup) sugar

70 ml (2½ fl ozs/generous ¼ cup) water

1 egg white

natural almond essence to taste (beware, 1 drop only!)

Coating

110 g (4 ozs/1 stick) melted butter

225 g (8 ozs/1 cup) castor sugar mixed with 4 rounded teasp. ground cinnamon. (This is approximate: the amount of the mixture depends on the size of the apples.)

To make the marzipan: Dissolve the sugar in the water and bring it to the boil. Cook to 116°C/240°F or to the 'soft ball' stage, keeping the sides of the saucepan brushed down with water. Remove from the heat and stir the syrup until cloudy. Add the ground almonds, essence and slightly-beaten egg whites. Mix very well. Turn into a bowl and allow it to become cool and firm. (Marzipan will keep for 3–4 weeks in a fridge.)

Meanwhile, peel and core the apples. Stuff the cavities with the marzipan filling. Roll the apples first in melted butter and then in the castor sugar and cinnamon. Place in an oven-proof dish and bake in a moderate oven, 180°C/350°F/regulo 4, for 1 hour approx.

Serve warm with a bowl of softly-whipped cream.

Bread and Butter Pudding

Serves 6–8

Bread and Butter Pudding is a most irresistible way of using up left-over white bread — this is a particularly delicious recipe.

12 slices good-quality white bread, crusts removed

55 g (2 ozs/½ stick) butter, preferably unsalted

½–1 teasp. freshly-grated nutmeg

200 g (7 ozs/1¼ cups) plump raisins *or* sultanas

455 ml (16 fl ozs/2 cups) cream

225 ml (8 fl ozs/1 cup) milk

4 large eggs, beaten lightly

1 teasp. pure vanilla essence

170 g (6 ozs/¾ cup) sugar

a pinch of salt

1 tablesp. (4 American teasp.) sugar for sprinkling on top of the pudding

Garnish

softly-whipped cream

1 x 20.5 cm (8 inches) square pottery *or* china dish

Butter the bread and arrange 4 slices, buttered side down, in one layer in the buttered dish. Sprinkle the bread with half the nutmeg and half the raisins, arrange another layer of bread, buttered side down, over the raisins, and sprinkle the remaining nutmeg and raisins on top. Cover the raisins with the remaining bread, buttered side down.

In a bowl whisk together the cream, milk, eggs, vanilla essence, sugar and a pinch of salt. Pour the mixture through a fine sieve over the bread. Sprinkle the sugar over the top and let the mixture stand, covered loosely, at room temperature for at least 1 hour or chill overnight.

Bake in a bain marie — the water should be half-way up the sides of the baking dish. Bake the pudding in the middle of a preheated oven, 180°C/350°F/regulo 4, for 1 hour approx. or until the top is crisp and golden. Serve the Pudding warm with some softly-whipped cream.

Note: This Bread and Butter Pudding reheats perfectly.

Winter Fruit Salad

SERVES 8

This slightly spicy dried fruit salad tastes marvellous in winter and has the great advantage that it keeps very well in the fridge. We serve it as a pudding but I've also been known to eat several bowls for breakfast!

185 g (6½ ozs/1 cup) prunes
170 g (6 ozs/1 cup) dried apricots
85 g (3 ozs/½ cup) raisins
2–3 pears
1–2 tablesp. (4–8 American teasp.) honey
grated rind of ½ lemon
12 walnut halves
½ vanilla pod
a small piece of cinnamon stick
2 cardamom pods (optional)
3–4 bananas
225 ml (8 fl ozs/1 cup) orange juice

Soak the prunes and apricots overnight in plenty of cold water. Next day, peel the pears and cut them in quarters. Put with the prunes, apricots, raisins, walnuts, lemon rind, vanilla pod, cinnamon stick and cardamom into a casserole. Mix the honey with 455 ml (16 fl ozs/2 cups) of the fruit-soaking water and pour over the prunes and apricots. Add a little more of the soaking water if the fruit is not covered. Cover, bring to the boil on top and simmer for 35 minutes approx. Alternatively, put into a moderate oven, 180°C/350°F/regulo 4.

Serve warm or cold. Just before serving, add a little fresh orange juice and some sliced bananas to each bowl. Serve with thick pouring cream.

This will keep for 1–2 weeks in a covered bowl in the fridge.

Fresh Fruit Salad
Serves 4

Many sins are committed in the name of fresh fruit salad. A really good fresh fruit salad can be so delicious and refreshing, particularly after a stew or casserole, but invariably it is bulked out with too much diced apple. This is a very simple fruit salad with ingredients available at any corner shop, but the principle can be used with other fruit as well.

It's very important when making a fruit salad to cut the fruit carefully into nicely shaped pieces.

1 ripe pear
1 ripe apple
2 ripe oranges
1 ripe banana
juice of 1 lemon
30 g (1 oz/generous ⅛ cup) approx. castor sugar

Optional extras
1 kiwi fruit
110 g (4 ozs) peeled and pipped green grapes

Peel the pear and apple, cut into quarters, core and cut across the grain into slices less than 5 mm (¼ inch) thick. Peel the orange with a stainless steel serrated knife as though you were peeling an apple, making sure to remove all the pith; then cut out each segment individually and add to the apple and pear. Sprinkle with castor sugar and lemon juice. About 15 minutes before serving, add the sliced bananas; taste and add more juice or sugar if necessary. If using kiwi fruit and grapes, add them with the orange.

Serve with a bowl of softly-whipped cream.

Note: The sugar and lemon juice will draw out the juice from the fruit and give a very fresh-tasting fruit salad.

Cakes for Christmas

The Christmas Cake is undoubtedly the 'cake of the year' as far as most people are concerned. Because of the expense of the ingredients a great deal of thought and preparation goes into the making and there is much discussion among friends about the 'best' recipe and how it should be followed. Often a favourite family recipe is handed down, but everyone swears by their own particular one. Well, I am offering you three alternatives in this book. Darina Allen's Christmas Cake is the recipe I have found most to my liking over the years. If you want to be really well organised it may of course be made weeks or even months ahead. I always thought a Christmas cake *had* to be made weeks ahead but when my children were small I often ended up frantically making it just days before Christmas and discovered to my great delight that it tasted even better that way! The Light Christmas Cake is also a great favourite of mine. My mother always cooked a Light Christmas Cake and a richer one every year and when my family gathered together on Christmas Eve we would all sit around a big fire with a pot of tea and Mum would cut the Light Cake. We're a huge family so my mother in fact baked twice the recipe and cooked it in a covered enamel roasting dish so there was plenty of 'cutting'. The White Christmas Cake which is an adaptation of a recipe given to me by my mother-in-law, Myrtle Allen, is iced with crisp Mountain Icing and is perfect for people who dislike traditional Christmas cakes. It doesn't keep so long but will certainly be delicious for up to two weeks.

Christmas wouldn't be complete without a Chocolate Yule Log; this is a really rich version and may indeed be served as a pudding also. It may be made several days ahead and provided it is kept covered with a damp cloth will keep perfectly and may be rolled up at the last minute.

Chapel Window Cake certainly takes some time to make and assemble but it has always been so much part of my childhood Christmas that I couldn't leave it out. Let your children help you to make it and I hope it will give them as much pleasure and excitement as it gave me.

Icing the cake is the bane of my life; first and foremost I'm not particularly fond of Royal Icing so there's no particular incentive to do miracles of wizardry on top of the cake; secondly, I'm not much good at it. I've been trying to work out why and I've decided that to be really good at cake icing you need to be patient because there is a good deal of waiting around for the icing to set at various stages. So invariably in my impatience to get the job finished I put the next layer on too soon and it runs off, or, horror of horrors, one colour runs into another. However you can get a very pleasing result with a simple design, and lots of deep red ribbon can cover a multitude of mistakes. I've given recipes for four icings here, all different and you can take your pick. I do want to draw your attention however, to Fondant Icing. This really is a tremendous breakthrough for those of us who find it all beyond us. The icing is simplicity itself to make, then you just roll it out and plonk it on the cake; it may be moulded into all sorts of shapes and flowers and coloured just like Royal Icing. There's only one slight drawback, it has virtually no flavour! However, if you brush it with gin or brandy before sticking it to the cake it improves the flavour no end!

Darina Allen's Christmas Cake with Toasted Almond Paste

This makes a moist cake which keeps very well. I have a passion for almond icing so I 'ice' the cake with almond icing and decorate it with heart shapes made from the Almond Paste. Then I brush it with beaten egg yolk and toast it in the oven — simply delicious!

225 g (8 ozs/2 sticks) butter
225 g (8 ozs/1 cup) pale, soft-brown sugar
6 eggs
285 g (10 ozs/2 cups) flour
1 teasp. mixed spice
70 ml (2½ fl ozs/generous ¼ cup) Irish whiskey
340 g (12 ozs/2 generous cups) best-quality sultanas
340 g (12 ozs/2 generous cups) best-quality currants
340 g (12 ozs/2 generous cups) best-quality raisins
110 g (4 ozs/½ cup) cherries
110 g (4 ozs/½ cup) home-made candied peel (see page 90)
55 g (2 ozs/scant ½ cup) whole almonds
55 g (2 ozs/generous ½ cup) ground almonds
rind of 1 lemon
rind of 1 orange
1 large or 2 small Bramley Seedling apples, grated

Line the base and sides of a 23 cm (9 inches) round, or a 20.5 cm (8 inches) square tin with brown paper and greaseproof paper.

Wash the cherries and dry them. Cut in two or four as desired. Blanch the almonds in boiling water for 1–2 minutes, rub off the skins and chop them finely. Mix the dried fruit, nuts, ground almonds and grated orange and lemon rind. Add about half the whiskey and leave for 1 hour to macerate.

Preheat the oven to 180°C/350°F/regulo 4. For fan or convection ovens, check the manufacturer's instructions for conversion.

Cream the butter until very soft, add the sugar and beat until light and fluffy. Whisk the eggs and add in bit by bit, beating well between each addition so that the mixture doesn't curdle. Mix the spice with the flour and *stir* in gently. Add the grated apple to the fruit and mix in gently but thoroughly (don't beat the mixture again or you will toughen the cake).

Put the mixture into the prepared cake tin. Make a slight hollow in the centre, dip your hand in water and pat it over the surface of the cake: this will ensure that the top is smooth when cooked. Put a sheet of greaseproof paper over the top of the tin; put into the preheated oven; reduce the heat to 160°C/325°F/regulo 3 after 1 hour. Bake until cooked; test in the centre with a skewer — it should come out completely clean, 3–3½ hours approx. Pour the rest of the whiskey over the cake and leave to cool in the tin.

Next day remove from the tin. Do not remove the lining paper but wrap in some extra greaseproof paper and tin foil until required.

Note: it is crucial to reduce the temperature by 10°–20° if using a fan oven, depending on the manufacturer's instructions.

Almond Paste

450 g (1 lb/4¾ cups) ground almonds
450 g (1 lb/4 cups) castor sugar
2 small eggs
a drop of pure almond essence
55 ml (2 tablesp./¼ cup) Irish whiskey

Sieve the castor sugar and mix with the ground almonds. Beat the eggs, add the whiskey and 1 drop of pure almond essence, then add to the other ingredients and mix to a stiff paste. (You may not need all the egg.) Sprinkle the work top with icing sugar, turn out the almond paste and work lightly until smooth.

To brush on the cake
1 egg white, lightly beaten

Glaze
2 egg yolks

Remove the paper from the cake. To make life easier for yourself, put a sheet of greaseproof paper onto the worktop; dust with some icing sugar. Take about half the almond paste and roll it out on the paper; it should be a little less than 1 cm (½ inch) thick. Paint the top of the cake with the lightly-beaten egg white and put the cake, sticky side down, onto the almond paste. Give the cake a 'thump' to make sure it sticks and then cut around the edge. If the cake is a little 'round shouldered' cut the almond paste a little larger; pull away the extra bits and keep for later to make hearts or holly leaves. With a palette knife press the extra almond paste in against the top of the cake to fill any gaps. Then slide a knife underneath the cake or, better still, underneath the paper and turn the cake right way up. Peel off the greaseproof paper.

Preheat the oven to 220°/425°F/regulo 7. For fan or convection ovens, check the manufacturers' instructions for conversion.

Next, measure the circumference of the cake with a piece of string. Roll out 2 long strips of almond paste; trim both edges to the height of the cake with a palette knife. Paint both the cake and the almond paste lightly with egg white. Press the strip against the sides of the cake: do not overlap or there will be a bulge. Use a straight-sided water glass to even the edges and smooth the join. Rub the cake well with your hand to ensure a nice flat surface. Roll out the remainder of the almond paste approx. 5 mm (¼ inch) thick. Cut out heart shapes, paint the whole surface of the cake with some beaten egg yolk, and stick the heart shapes at intervals around the sides of the cake and on the top. Brush these with egg yolk also.

Carefully lift the cake onto a baking sheet and bake in the preheated oven for 15–20 minutes or until just slightly toasted. Remove from the oven, allow to cool and then transfer onto a cake board.

Note: As I'm an incurable romantic, my Christmas Cake is always decorated with hearts, but you may well feel that holly leaves and berries made of almond paste would be more appropriate for Christmas! Basically, you can of course decorate it any way that takes your fancy.

Light Christmas Cake

225 g (8 ozs/2 sticks) butter
225 g (8 ozs/1 generous cup) castor sugar
4 large *or* 5 small eggs
285 g (10 ozs/2 cups) flour
55 g (2 ozs/generous ½ cup) ground almonds
55 g (2 ozs/scant ½ cup) whole almonds
a pinch of salt
⅛ teasp. breadsoda dissolved in 1 teasp. milk
grated rind of 1 orange
200 g (7 ozs/1 generous cup) sultanas
200 g (7 ozs/1 generous cup) raisins
55 g (2 ozs/¼ cup) currants
110 g (4 ozs/½ cup) home-made chopped candied peel (see page 90)
55 g (2 ozs/generous ¼ cup) cherries, cut in quarters

Preheat the oven to 150°C/300°F/regulo 2. For fan or convection ovens, check the manufacturer's instructions for conversion.

Line the base and sides of a 20.5 cm (8 inches) diameter x 7.5 cm (3 inches) high round cake tin with greaseproof and brown paper.

Blanch the whole almonds in boiling water for 1 or 2 minutes, rub off the skins and chop. Mix all the fruit together with the cherries, peel, ground and chopped almonds. Cream the butter until really soft, add in the castor sugar and beat until light and creamy. Whisk the eggs and add in bit by bit, beating well between each addition. Add the grated orange rind, *stir* in the flour and all of the fruit. Dissolve the breadsoda in the milk and stir thoroughly through the mixture. Spoon into the prepared tin and bake in the preheated oven for 2½–3 hours. Allow to get cold, turn out of the tin and wrap in greaseproof paper until ready to ice.

Almond Icing

225 g (8 ozs/2 generous cups) ground almonds
225 g (8 ozs/2 cups) icing sugar
225 g (8 ozs/1 generous cup) castor sugar
1 egg
1 tablesp. (4 American teasp.) lemon juice
1 tablesp. (4 American teasp.) whiskey
1 egg white, slightly beaten

Note: This is a milder almond icing than the one used for Darina Allen's Cake but the two are interchangeable. (Use half the quantity given on page 61.)

Put the ground almonds and sugars into a bowl. Beat the egg lightly with the whiskey and lemon juice: make a well in the centre of the almonds and stir in the liquid, keeping a little back at first in case it's not all needed. Mix to a stiff paste.

Remove the paper from the cake. To make life easier for yourself, put a sheet of greaseproof paper onto the work top; dust with some icing sugar. Take about half the almond paste and roll it out on the paper: it should be a little less than 1 cm (½ inch) thick. Paint the top of the cake with the lightly-beaten egg white and put the cake, sticky side down, onto the almond paste. Give the cake a 'thump' to make sure it sticks and then cut around the edge. If the cake is a little 'round shouldered' cut the almond paste a little larger; pull away the extra bits and keep for the sides. With a palette knife press the extra almond paste in against the top of the cake to fill any gaps. Then slide a knife underneath the cake or, better still, underneath the paper and turn the cake right way up. Peel off the greaseproof paper.

Next, measure the circumference of the cake with a piece of string. Roll out 2 long strips of almond paste; trim both edges to the height of the cake with a palette knife. Paint both the cake and the almond paste lightly with egg white. Press the strip against the sides of the cake: do not overlap or there will be a bulge. Use a straight-sided water glass to even the edges and smooth the join. Rub the cake well with your hand to ensure a nice flat surface. Leave the cake to dry overnight before applying Royal or Fondant Icing.

Royal Icing

450 g (1 lb/4 cups) icing sugar
2 egg whites
2 teasp. strained lemon juice

Whisk the egg whites in a large bowl just until they begin to froth; then add the sieved icing sugar by the tablespoonful, beating well between each addition. If you are making it in an electric mixer, use the lowest speed. When all the icing sugar has been incorporated, add the lemon juice, and if you would like a slightly soft icing add a few drops of glycerine. Beat until the icing reaches stiff peaks; scrape down the sides of the bowl. Cover the bowl with a damp cloth for 1 hour or until you are ready to use the icing.

Clockwise from left
Chapel Window Cake; White Christmas Cake; Chocolate Yule Log

Darina Allen's Christmas Cake with Toasted Almond Paste

Fondant Icing

Darina Allen's Christmas Cake with Royal Icing

Chocolate Christmas Tree

With the help of a flexible palette knife, smear the icing over the top and sides of the cake. For the least skilled of us, the simplest finish for a Christmas cake is the snow-scene effect. This is easily achieved by dabbing the palette knife onto the cake at irregular intervals so the icing comes up in little peaks. While the icing is still wet, stick on some Christmas cake decorations, e.g. Santas, Christmas trees and robins. If you want to be more ambitious, spread a thinner layer of icing onto the cake so that the top and sides are as smooth as possible. Cover the remainder of the icing with a damp cloth; leave the cake in a cool place or overnight to allow the first coat of icing to set.

With a small star nozzle, pipe rosettes or shell shapes around the top and base of the cake. Tie a red ribbon around the sides and tie in a flat bow. Decorate the top with rosettes in a star shape or in the shape of a Christmas tree — or you might have a go at writing Merry Christmas. Best of luck — have fun and Merry Christmas to you too!

Fondant Icing

MAKES 620 G (1 LB 6 OZS) APPROX.

Fondant Icing has taken the confectionery business by storm; it's so easy to make and roll out that simply anybody can ice a cake with it. We have the Australians to thank for this wonderfully versatile icing. They were apparently having a bad time trying to get our Royal Icing to work in their various climates. Some areas were far too hot so the icing was rock hard in no time; other areas were too humid so the icing refused to set. So some 'clever clogs' developed this icing which is sometimes referred to as sugar paste or 'ready to roll'. Liquid glucose is an essential ingredient in Fondant Icing.

450 g (1 lb/4 cups) icing sugar
1 egg white
25 ml (2 rounded tablesp./8 teasp.) liquid glucose
1 teasp. glycerine
1 teasp. lemon juice or orange flower water

Fondant may be made either in a food processor or by hand. If you are using a processor, put the icing sugar into the bowl first and then the egg white, liquid glucose, glycerine and lemon juice or orange flower water. Whizz until mixed. Stop and scrape the mixture from the sides if necessary and whizz again. It is also very quick to make fondant by hand. Just put all the ingredients into a large bowl, gradually mix the icing sugar into the wet ingredients with one hand, holding the bowl steady with the other.

Turn the fondant out onto a clean work top, lightly dredged with sieved icing sugar. Knead until smooth, using a little more icing sugar if necessary but not too much. Otherwise the fondant will be dry and liable to crack. If you would like to add colour, put it in with a cocktail stick at this stage. Knead in the colour evenly. Keep it wrapped in polythene when not in use.

To cover the cake with fondant icing: Fondant Icing may be applied directly onto a cake. If the surface is uneven, you might like to smooth it out with some little bits of fondant first, then paint the surface of the cake with a little lightly-beaten egg white and apply the fondant. However, I prefer to put a thin layer of almond paste on first (see page 61). Allow the almond paste to dry at least overnight and preferably for 2 or 3 days. Brush the almond paste all over with a little brandy, whiskey or rum.

Roll out the fondant 5 mm (¼ inch) approx. thick, brush with chosen spirit as above and carefully lift it onto the cake, making sure not to trap air under the icing. Press onto the surface of the cake with your hand. Air bubbles will form under the fondant; prick these with a darning needle and press the air out. Smooth and polish the fondant with the palm of your hand. This will make the cake smooth and shiny. Trim the base of the cake; the trimmings may be used to make stars or holly leaves and berries. Use a crimpers to decorate the edges.

If you would like to 'posh' up the bottom, you can make a very effective frill quite easily, but first mark the cake all the way around with pin pricks 2.5 cm (1 inch) from the base. Roll out the trimmings of the fondant thinly and stamp out one fluted round 7.5 cm diameter (3 inches). Cover the rest. Cut a circle out of the centre of the round with a 4 cm (1½ inch) cutter. Using a cocktail stick, roll the fluted edge to thin it out; it will begin to look like a frill. Cut the circular frill so you can open it out to form a straight piece. Brush the pin pricks on the cake sparingly with water. Carefully lift the frill and press the straight edge onto the cake just above the 'pin prick'. Adjust the frill and neaten with a skewer or handle of a child's paint brush. Continue to make frills until the base is covered. Tie a wide red ribbon around the cake and decorate the top with fondant holly leaves and berries and some Christmas cake decorations.

White Christmas Cake

This White Christmas Cake with its layer of crisp frosting is a delicious alternative for those who do not like the traditional fruit cake. It is best made not more than a week before Christmas.

140 g (5 ozs/1¼ stick) butter
200 g (7 ozs/1½ cups) flour
¼ teasp. baking powder
a pinch of salt
1 teasp. Irish whiskey
1 teasp. lemon juice
85 g (3 ozs/1 cup) ground almonds
6 egg whites
225 g (8 ozs/1 generous cup) castor sugar
85–110 g (3–4 ozs/½ cup) green *or* yellow cherries
55 g (2 ozs/¼ cup) finely-chopped home-made candied peel (see page 90)

White frosting
1 egg white
225 g (8 ozs/1 generous cup) granulated sugar
4 tablesp. (16 American teasp.) water

1 x 18 cm (7 inches) round tin with 7.5 cm (3 inches) sides

Preheat the oven to 160°C/325°F/regulo 3. For fan or convection ovens, check the manufacturer's instructions for conversion.

Line the tin with greaseproof paper. Cream the butter until very soft, sieve in the flour, salt and baking powder, then add the lemon juice, whiskey and ground almonds. Whisk the egg whites until quite stiff; add the castor sugar gradually and whisk again until stiff and smooth. Stir some of the egg white into the butter mixture and then carefully fold in the rest. Lastly, add the chopped peel and the halved cherries. Pour into the prepared tin and bake for 1½ hours approx. Allow to cool, cover and ice the next day.

To make the white frosting: This delicious icing is just a little tricky to make, so follow the instructions exactly. Quick and accurate decisions are necessary in judging when the icing is ready and then it must be used immediately. Whisk the egg white until very stiff in a pyrex or pottery bowl. Dissolve the sugar carefully in water and boil for 1½ minutes approx. until the syrup reaches the 'thread stage', 106°–113°C/223°–236°F. It will look thick and syrupy; when a metal spoon is dipped in, the last drops of syrup will form a thin thread. Pour this boiling syrup over the stiffly-beaten egg white, whisking all the time. Put the bowl in a saucepan over simmering water. Continue to whisk over the water until white and very thick (this can take up to 10 minutes). Spread quickly over the cake with a palette knife. It sets very quickly at this stage, so speed is essential.

Decorate with Christmas decorations or crystallised violets or rose petals and angelica.

Chocolate Yule Log
SERVES 10 APPROX.

Chocolate Yule Log is usually made with a chocolate sponge Swiss Roll but I prefer this sinfully rich version. There's no need for any icing, it's rich enough as it is!

170 g (6 ozs) best-quality dark chocolate
5 eggs
170 g (6 ozs/1 scant cup) castor sugar
3 tablesp. (4 American tablesp.) water

Filling
285 ml (½ pint/1¼ cups) double cream
1–2 tablesp. (4–8 American teasp.) rum
icing sugar

1 x shallow Swiss roll tin 30.5 cm (12 inches) x 20.5 cm (8 inches)

Preheat the oven to 180°C/350°F/regulo 4. For fan or convection ovens, check the manufacturer's instructions for conversion.

Line a Swiss roll tin with oiled tin foil. Separate the eggs. Put the yolks into a bowl, gradually add the castor sugar and whisk until the mixture is thick and pale lemon coloured. Melt the chocolate with the water in a saucepan over a very gentle heat, then draw aside while you whisk the egg whites to a firm snow. Add the melted chocolate to the egg yolk mixture. Stir a little of the egg white into the mixture, cut and fold the remainder of the egg whites into the mixture and turn it into the prepared tin. Cook in a preheated oven, bake for 15–18 minutes or until firm to the touch around the edge but still slightly soft in the centre. Wring out a tea-towel in cold water. Take out the roulade, cool it slightly, then cover with the cloth. (This is to prevent any sugary crust forming.) Leave it in a cool place. Provided the cloth is kept damp, it will keep for 2 days like this.

To serve: Whip the cream and flavour with the rum. Put a sheet of greaseproof paper onto a table and dust it well with sieved icing sugar. Remove the damp cloth from the roulade and turn the tin upside down onto the prepared paper. Remove the tin and peel the tin foil off the roulade carefully. Spread with the rum-flavoured cream and roll it up like a Swiss Roll. Cut about one-third off the roll at an angle. Lift the roll onto a serving plate, arrange the smaller piece so it looks like a branch and dust well with icing sugar. Decorate with Christmas cake decorations, e.g. holly leaves, Santas, robins etc., sprinkle again with a little extra icing sugar and serve.

Chapel Window Cake

Mummy used to make this cake for us every Christmas; we would all gather round as children and watch in rapt amazement as she assembled it. We simply couldn't wait to get a taste and there were always dreadful squabbles about the end bits which were cut off to make the cake look even. Much to our annoyance, the cake itself was usually put away in a tin for several days before being cut.

170 g (6 ozs/1½ sticks) butter
170 g (6 ozs/scant 1 cup) castor sugar
225 g (8 ozs/scant 2 cups) flour
4 eggs
1 teasp. baking powder
¼ teasp. pure vanilla essence
rind of ½ lemon
natural pink colouring
1 drop pure almond essence
30 g (1 oz) drinking chocolate powder
25 ml (1 tablesp./⅛ cup) milk
¼ teasp. pure vanilla essence
home-made raspberry *or* apricot jam

Almond paste
225 g (8 ozs/scant 2½ cups) ground almonds
225 g (8 ozs/2 cups) castor sugar
1 small egg
a drop of pure almond essence (optional)
25 ml (1 tablesp./⅛ cup) Irish whiskey

Preheat the oven to 190°C/375°F/regulo 5. For fan or convection ovens, check the manufacturer's instructions for conversion.

Line 3 loaf tins, 19 cm (7½ inches) x 11.5 cm (4½ inches), with greaseproof paper. Cream the butter until really soft, add in the castor sugar and beat until white and fluffy. Whisk the eggs and beat in bit by bit. Sieve the flour with the baking powder and *stir* into the mixture.

Divide the mixture into 3 equal parts. Flavour one part with grated lemon rind; add a few drops of pink colouring and 1 drop of pure almond essence to the second; blend chocolate powder with the milk, add vanilla essence and fold into the third mixture. Fill individually into the prepared tins and bake in a preheated oven for 20 minutes approx. or until firm to the touch. Cool on a wire rack.

Meanwhile make the almond paste. Sieve the sugar and mix with the ground almonds. Beat the eggs, add 1 drop of pure almond essence, add to the other ingredients and mix to a stiff paste. (You may not need all the egg.) Sprinkle the work top with icing sugar, turn out the almond paste and work lightly until smooth.

When the cakes are cold, trim the edges slightly and cut each one into four lengthways. Brush all over the sides with raspberry or apricot jam. Put the pieces together so that the colours in each line — both up and down — are different. Press well together. This is a sticky job, so it may be necessary to wash your hands at this stage!

Put a sheet of silicone paper on the work top and sprinkle with icing sugar. Roll out the almond paste into an oblong 20.5 cm (8 inches) x 12.5 cm (5 inches) and 5 mm (¼ inch) approx. thick.

Spread some jam on the base of the cake. Place it quarter way down the oblong of almond paste. Paint the sides of the cake with jam, lift up the paper under the first quarter of almond paste and stick the almond paste to the cake. Flip over the cake so the almond paste sticks to the third side. Finally brush jam on the last side and lift up the paper so that the almond paste will stick to the cake. Press the edges well together and smooth with your hand. Turn the cake over so that the join is underneath. Mark the top into squares with a blunt knife and pinch the edges.

Trim the ends and eat them with a cup of tea or coffee — you will certainly deserve them after all that! This cake keeps for a week or 10 days in an airtight tin. Use any scraps of left-over almond paste to make Marzipan Dates (see page 88).

Entertaining

In this section there are some recipes for little 'bites' to go with drinks and several recipes for home-made lemonade. If you keep a jar of stock syrup in your fridge it takes only a matter of minutes to make lemonade — children can make it themselves and they absolutely love it for school lunches. The Fruit Punch is non-alcoholic and makes a delicious thirst-quenching drink for a party. Toby's Hot Chocolate is really delicious, easy to make and exquisitely rich; I can hardly imagine that it could be improved, but I am reliably told by some Quaker friends that if one adds a tablespoon of Jamaica rum to a mug of hot chocolate it becomes a Lumumba — a very cheering drink indeed! Speaking of cheering drinks, don't forget to offer lots of Irish spring water if you are having a drinks party around Christmas. The Mulled Wine is easy to make and looks great served in a big punch bowl; the Mince Pies may be made ahead but should be cooked just at the last minute, so they are served warm. If you would like to offer additional food, I've suggested lots of other little 'bites'. Make sure everything tastes really good: all too often at drinks parties food looks stunning but tastes rather less so. Make sure that each bite is well-seasoned and looks appetising.

Mulled Red Wine

SERVES 8 APPROX.

One of the easiest ways to entertain some of your friends before Christmas is to serve Mulled Wine and Mince Pies with lots of Whiskey Cream. At that stage they are still a novelty, whereas after Christmas people tend to groan, 'Oh no, not Mince Pies again!'

1 bottle of good red wine
110 g (4 ozs/1 cup) sugar
thinly-pared rind of 1 lemon
a small piece of cinnamon bark
a blade of mace
1 clove

Put the sugar into a stainless steel or cast-iron saucepan, pour the wine over, add the lemon rind, cinnamon bark, mace and the clove. Heat slowly, stirring to make sure the sugar is dissolved. When it is hot but not scalding serve in glasses with a wedge of lemon in each one if desired.

Irish Whiskey Punch
Serves 1

This most warming beverage is guaranteed to restore your spirits if you feel a cold coming on! Even if you don't, try it anyway — nothing could be more comforting to sip by a roaring fire on a winter's evening.

70 ml (2½ fl ozs/¼ cup) Irish whiskey
1 segment of lemon
3 *or* 4 cloves
2 teasp. sugar
boiling water

Put the whiskey and sugar into a robust glass, stick the cloves into the segment of lemon and add; fill to the top with boiling water; stir to dissolve the sugar. Serve immediately.

Fruit Punch
Makes 30 glasses approx.

900 g (2 lbs/4½ cups) sugar
2.3 L (4 pints/10 cups) water
4 sweet geranium leaves (optional)
4 mandarins *or* clementines, peeled and thinly sliced
10 oranges
6 lemons *or* 4 lemons and 2 limes
4 bananas
285 g (10 ozs) small seedless grapes
1.1. L (2 pints/5 cups) ginger ale
570 ml (1 pint /2½ cups) cold strained tea
2.3 L (4 pints /10 cups) soda water

Garnish
Sprigs of fresh mint *or* lemon balm

Put the sugar and sweet geranium leaves (if using) into a saucepan, cover with cold water and bring to the boil; simmer for 5 minutes. Allow it to cool slightly, then add the peeled and thinly-sliced mandarins or clementines. Juice the oranges, lemons and limes. Remove the sweet geranium leaves from the cold syrup; add the fruit juice, grapes and sliced bananas. Chill thoroughly, then add the ginger ale, cold tea and soda water. Just before serving, add lots of ice.

Serve in a large punch bowl with sprigs of fresh mint or lemon balm floating on top.

Home-made Lemonades

All these fresh fruit drinks are simplicity itself to make, particularly if you keep some chilled 'stock syrup' made up in your fridge. However, they contain no preservatives so they should be served within a few hours of being made.

Stock syrup
450 g (1 lb/2 cups) sugar
570 ml (1 pint/2½ cups) water

To make stock syrup: Dissolve the sugar in the water and bring to the boil. Boil for 2 minutes then allow it to cool. Store in the fridge until needed.

Lemonade

4 lemons
285 ml (½ pint/1¼ cups) stock syrup
700 ml (1¼ pints/3 cups) water
ice-cubes

Garnish
Sprigs of fresh mint *or* lemon balm

Juice the lemons and add the syrup and water. Taste and add a little more water or syrup if necessary. Add ice, garnish with sprigs of fresh mint or lemon balm and serve.

Lemon and Limeade

4 lemons
1 lime
700 ml (1¼ pints/3 cups) water
285 ml (½ pint/1¼ cups) stock syrup
ice-cubes

Garnish
Sprigs of fresh mint *or* lemon balm

Make and serve as above. Taste and add more water if necessary.

Orange and Lemonade

3 oranges
2 lemons
140 ml (¼ pint/½ cup) stock syrup
425–570 ml (¾–1 pint/2–2½ cups) water
ice-cubes

Garnish
Sprigs of fresh mint *or* lemon balm

Make and serve as above. Taste and adjust if necessary.

Toby's Hot Chocolate
Serves 4

This is the recipe for Hot Chocolate that my son Toby makes. It's wickedly rich and absolutely scrumptious: the flavour of 'proper' hot chocolate is a revelation if you've never tried it before.

100–110 g (3½–4 ozs) best-quality dark chocolate
70 ml (2½ fl ozs/8 American teasp.) water
570 ml (1 pint/2½ cups) milk
1–2 teasp. sugar
4 large teasp. (8 American teasp.) whipped cream
grated chocolate

Put the chocolate and water into a heavy saucepan and melt on a very low heat. Meanwhile, bring the milk almost to the boil (what we call the 'shivery' stage) in a separate saucepan. When the chocolate has melted, pour on the milk, whisking all the time; it should be smooth and frothy. Taste and add some sugar. Pour it into warmed cups, spoon a blob of whipped cream on top and sprinkle with a little grated chocolate.

EATS FOR DRINKS

Smoked Cod's Roe on Toast with Sour Cream and Chives
ALLOW 1–2 PER PERSON

Smoked cod's roe is available from August to March. At first it seems very salty and indeed it is, but it is addictive; the only disadvantage is that it makes you very thirsty, so perhaps it's not the best thing for a drinks party after all!

Ovals or rounds of toast or crisp croûtons
smoked cod's roe
sour cream or fromage blanc

Garnish
finely-chopped chives
freshly-ground pepper

Spread some cod's roe on each piece of toast or crouton. Top with a tiny blob of sour cream or fromage blanc. Sprinkle with freshly-chopped chives and a few turns of the pepper mill.

Note: Fromage blanc is a fresh cheese made from skimmed milk and is low in calories. It is now fairly widely available in supermarkets.

Cockles or Mussels with Mayonnaise
ALLOW 2 PER PERSON

cockles or mussels
home-made mayonnaise (*Simply Delicious*, page 4)

Garnish
Sprigs of fennel or flat parsley

Check that all the cockles or mussels are tightly shut. Wash them under lots of cold running water. Put them in a single layer in a wide frying pan. Cover with a folded tea-towel and cook on a gentle heat for 1–2 minutes. As soon as they open, remove the tea-towel. If you are using mussels, remove the beards and leave the mussels or cockles on a half shell. Allow them to get quite cold. Loosen the mussels or cockles from the shell, pipe a tiny rosette of mayonnaise on each one and decorate with a sprig of fennel or flat parsley.

Prawns wrapped in Spinach Leaves
ALLOW 2 PER PERSON APPROX.

freshly-cooked Dublin Bay prawns
tender spinach leaves
home-made mayonnaise *or* garlic mayonnaise (*Simply Delicious*, pages 4 and 5)

Garnish
fennel *or* flat parsley

Blanch and refresh the spinach leaves, then spread them out on kitchen paper.

To assemble: Spread a little mayonnaise on a spinach leaf and place a cooked Dublin Bay prawn in the centre. Roll up into a tiny parcel, repeat with all the prawns. Chill. Garnish with fennel or flat parsley and serve.

Note: Cooked mussels or shrimps may also be used in this recipe; lettuce leaves could be substituted for spinach.

Tiny Smoked Salmon Sandwiches
MAKES 24

12 slices Ballymaloe brown yeast bread (*Simply Delicious*, page 74)
12 thin pieces of smoked Irish salmon
freshly-ground pepper
lemon

Garnish
tiny sprigs of fresh fennel *or* dill

Butter the slices of bread and make a double-decker sandwich with the smoked salmon. Season each layer with freshly-ground pepper and a few drops of lemon juice, then butter the top of the sandwich. Trim a slice of smoked salmon to fit the top exactly, and press down onto the butter. Then trim off the crusts and cut the sandwiches into 6 tiny squares.

Garnish each one with a tiny sprig of fresh fennel or dill and serve.

Celery Sticks stuffed with Cashel Blue Cheese
ALLOW 1 PER PERSON

We use Cashel Blue for this recipe but other blue cheese may also be used. Taste; you may have to adjust the proportion of butter depending on the saltiness of the cheese.

1 crisp head of celery
110 g (4 ozs) Cashel Blue cheese
55 g (2 ozs/½ stick) butter (preferably unsalted)
freshly-ground pepper

Garnish
chopped spring onion

Purée the Cashel Blue cheese and butter together. Taste and season with freshly-ground pepper. Spread this cheese mixture into the hollows of the sticks of celery. Leave whole if the sticks are small, otherwise cut into 4 cm (1½ inch) chunks diagonally. Arrange on napkin-lined baskets. Sprinkle with chopped spring onion.

Note: This cheese mixture may also be piped or spread onto tiny crackers and garnished with a sprig of flat parsley or chervil.

Cucumber Boats stuffed with Tapenade
MAKES 20–24 PIECES APPROX.

Tapenade will keep for several weeks in a covered jar in the fridge; it is also wonderful served as a dip with raw vegetables.

1 cucumber

Tapenade
55 g (2 ozs) anchovy fillets
100 g (3½ ozs/½ cup) stoned black olives
20 g (1 tablesp./4 teasp.) capers
1 teasp. mustard
1 teasp. lemon juice
1 tablesp. (4 American teasp.) brandy (optional)
freshly-ground pepper
37 ml (2–3 tablesp./scant ¼ cup) olive oil

First make the tapenade. Whiz up the anchovy fillets (preferably in a food processor) with the stoned black olives, capers, mustard, lemon juice, brandy and pepper. Alternatively, use a pestle and mortar. When it becomes a smooth purée, add the olive oil.

Peel the cucumbers, halve and remove the seeds with a melon baler or a teaspoon. Spoon the tapenade into the centre of each cucumber boat, cover with cling-film and refrigerate for about 1 hour, so the cucumbers will be crisp and easy to slice. Cut into 3 cm (1¼ inch) pieces with a sharp knife, arrange on a plate and serve.

Stuffed Red and Yellow Cherry Tomatoes

Delicious little red and yellow cherry tomatoes are now available almost all year round in the shops. They make perfect canapés if you have the patience to scoop out the centres and may be stuffed with many different fillings.

red and yellow cherry tomatoes

Cut a slice off the round end of the cherry tomatoes and scoop out the seeds with a small melon-baller. Fill with your chosen filling and replace the lid. Serve on a plate lined with dark green lettuce leaves. Garnish with watercress.

Filling of your choice:
1. Tapenade (see page 77)
2. Cream cheese with finely-chopped fresh mint
3. Cold cooked fish or shellfish, e.g. salmon, trout, shrimps, prawns etc. mixed with French dressing and fresh herbs or mayonnaise and fresh herbs
4. Cold scrambled egg with chives
5. Fromage blanc with chives or dill

Pâté on Water Biscuits
MAKES 24–30 BISCUITS

Use the Smooth Turkey Liver Pâté recipe given on page 11.

225 g (8 ozs/generous 1½ cups) flour
½ teasp. salt
1 teasp. (1 American teasp.) baking powder
55 g (2 ozs/½ stick) butter
water
sea salt for sprinkling on top

Preheat the oven to 180°C/350°F/regulo 4.

Sieve the flour, salt and baking powder into a bowl, cut the butter into cubes and rub into the flour. Add enough water to mix to a firm dough. Shape into a ball and roll out on a lightly-floured board to a thickness of about 3 mm (⅛ inch). Prick all over with a fork. Stamp out into 4 cm (1½ inch) rounds. Sprinkle with sea salt and bake in a preheated moderate oven for 35–45 minutes or until they turn a pale golden colour. Cool on a wire rack. Pipe rosettes of pâté onto the biscuits and garnish with a tiny piece of tomato concassé and a sprig of chervil.

These biscuits store well in an airtight tin. If you would like to serve them with cheese, stamp out into 9 cm (3½ inch) rounds.

Scrambled Egg with Chives and Smoked Salmon
MAKES 24 APPROX.

Cold Scrambled Egg with Chives may not strike you as being in the least appetising! Try it, it makes the very best egg sandwiches, and served here on tiny croutons with little strips of smoked salmon on top, it makes a delicious cocktail bite.

2 eggs
1 tablesp. (4 American teasp.) cream *or* milk
a dot of butter
salt and freshly-ground pepper
1 teasp. finely-chopped chives
sprigs of watercress
trimmings of smoked salmon cut in strips
squares of brown bread *or* toast

Garnish
chopped chives *or* watercress

Scramble the eggs in the usual way, add the chives, taste for seasoning and allow to get quite cold.

To assemble: Put a tiny teaspoon of scrambled egg on 4 cm (1½ inch) rounds or croutons or similar-sized square pieces of brown bread. Sprinkle with strips of smoked salmon. Garnish with chopped chives or watercress.

Salted Almonds

SERVES 8 APPROX.

225 g (8 ozs/1½ cups) whole almonds
oil
sea salt

Preheat the oven to moderate, 180°C/350°F/regulo 4.

Bring a small saucepan of water to the boil, toss in the almonds and boil for
1 or 2 minutes. Strain. Put the almonds in a tea-towel and rub off the skins.
Put the peeled almonds onto a lightly-oiled Swiss roll tin and place in the
preheated oven. They should be nicely golden in about 20 minutes. Sprinkle
with sea salt.

From front
Mince Pies; Toby's Hot Chocolate; Kumquats in Brandy

From left

Salted Almonds; Scrambled Egg with Chives and Smoked Salmon; Cucumber Boats stuffed with Tapenade; Celery Sticks stuffed with Cashel Blue Cheese; Tiny Smoked Salmon Sandwiches; Pâté on Water Biscuits; Stuffed Red Cherry Tomatoes; Mussels with Mayonnaise; Prawns wrapped in Spinach Leaves; Salted Almonds

From left

Ginger Christmas Tree Biscuits; Vanilla Moons; Checkerboard Biscuits; Hazelnut Sticks; Holy Biscuits; Almond Macaroons; Pinwheel Biscuits; Almond Crisps; 'S' Biscuits

Top row from left
Doreen's Fudge; Pickled Kumquats with Orange Slices; Orange, Lemon and Grapefruit Marmalade;
Marzipan Dates
Bottom row from left
Kumquats in Brandy; Christmas Tree Biscuits; Ballymaloe Mincemeat; Raspberry Jam *(Simply
Delicious)*

Plate on left

Mary Jo's Chocolates; Chocolate Fruit and Nuts; Chocolate Truffles rolled in Praline; Chocolate Truffles rolled in Cocoa; Mary Jo's Chocolates

Edible Presents

One of the great secrets of a happy Christmas, it seems to me, is to get the whole family involved in the preparations; rope everyone in, children, grannies, grandads and any spare aunt or uncle you can find. If everyone talks about it then the build-up of excitement is tremendous — this is what memories are made of! Plans could get underway good and early so that there's minimum last-minute frazzle. Children adore being part of the action and with a minimum of encouragement and perhaps a very little adult supervision (sometimes it's better not to look!), they can produce really charming Christmas cards. It may be a little messy but on the other hand they will be happy for hours and the end result will delight everyone who gets one and an extra bonus will be quite a saving on 'bought' cards. Children learn the very important lesson that cards or presents which one puts time into and makes one's self are in many ways of greater value than expensive knick-knacks bought at the last minute in the shops. For this reason I have put a Christmas Biscuits section into this book specially to encourage the lovely Austrian and German tradition of making special Christmas biscuits to give as presents to family and friends. All these biscuits keep for ages in an airtight tin, so you could start at the beginning of December and make one kind at a time for several weeks. Children or teenagers can make them almost unaided and for a few pounds worth of ingredients enough biscuits can be produced to give presents to half the neighbourhood. The look of pride on your children's faces as they wrap their plates of home-made biscuits will be enough to remind you of the real spirit of Christmas!

Also in this section is a recipe for a really stunning Chocolate Christmas Tree which is the greatest fun to make. It looks so lovely you won't want to eat it. Mary Jo's Chocolates, Fudge, Marzipan Dates and Pamelas could make up a lovely box of home-made chocolates. The Palestrina Christmas Cake may be made months ahead of Christmas and is a wonderful confection packed solid with fruit and nuts.

Home-made Jam, Marmalade or Chutney is always given a great welcome. Cover the jars prettily and ask the children to do special labels such as 'for my granny with love'.

Ballymaloe Mincemeat

MAKES 3.15 KG (7 LBS) APPROX.

2 cooking apples, e.g. Bramley Seedling
2 lemons
450 g (1 lb/4 cups) beef suet
110 g (4 ozs/½ cup) mixed peel (preferably home-made)
2 tablesp. (8 American teasp.) orange marmalade (see page 88)
225 g (8 ozs/1½ cups) currants
450 g (1 lb/2¼ cups) raisins
225 g (8 ozs/1½ cups) sultanas
900 g (2 lbs/4 cups) Barbados sugar (moist, soft, dark-brown sugar)
70 ml (2½ fl ozs/generous ¼ cup) Irish whiskey

Core and bake the whole apples in a moderate oven, 180°C/350°F/regulo 4, for 45 minutes approx. When they are soft, remove the skin and mash the flesh into pulp. Grate the rind from the lemons on the finest part of a stainless steel grater and squeeze out the juice. Add the other ingredients one by one, and as they are added, mix everything thoroughly together. Put into jars, cover with jam covers and leave to mature for 2 weeks before using. This mincemeat will keep for months or a year in a cool, airy place.

Note: If the mincemeat is for presents, put white doyleys over the jam covers and tie with red and green ribbons.

Kumquats in Brandy

500 g (1 lb 2 ozs) kumquats
450 g (1 lb/2 cups) sugar
750 ml (1¼ pint/1 bottle) brandy

Wash the kumquats and prick them all over; a sterilised darning needle is the perfect implement. Put them into a sterilised screw-top jar with the sugar, pour over a bottle of brandy and screw on the lid. Reverse the jar so that the sugar begins to dissolve, and continue to reverse every day for 2–3 weeks. After 4 weeks the liqueur will be ready to drink. The kumquats are delicious eaten with home-made vanilla ice-cream or just with cream.

Divide into smaller sterilised jars for presents, cover and label attractively.

Pickled Kumquats with Orange Slices

MAKES 1–2 JARS, DEPENDING ON SIZE

This delicious pickle comes from Jane Grigson's *Fruit Book*; I give it to you with her permission. It is delicious served with cold ham, goose, duck or pork.

225 g (8 ozs) kumquats
1 large orange
285 g (10 ozs/1¼ cups) sugar
225 ml (8 fl ozs/1 cup) white wine vinegar
5 cm (2 inches) piece of cinnamon stick
8 whole cloves
2 blades of mace

Scrub the orange well and rinse the kumquats. Cut a slice off the top and bottom of the orange down as far as the flesh and discard those two pieces of peel. Cut the rest of the orange into slices and put them in a wide stainless steel saucepan with the kumquats. Cover generously with cold water. Bring to the boil, cover and simmer until the orange slices are tender, 20–30 minutes approx. The kumquats may be ready before the orange slices so keep an eye on them and remove them if they show signs of collapsing.

Meanwhile in a stainless steel saucepan dissolve the sugar in the white wine vinegar, add the cinnamon, cloves and mace, and stir until it comes to the boil. Drain all the liquid off the oranges and keep aside in case you need it. Put the kumquats and oranges into the vinegar syrup and if necessary use some of the cooking liquid to cover the fruit. Simmer until the orange slices look transparent and slightly candied, 15 minutes approx.

Arrange the fruit in a wide-mouthed sterilised glass jar, pour the boiling syrup over and cover tightly (*not* with a tin lid). Label and leave to mature for 3–4 weeks before use.

Kumquat Jam

MAKES 3 SMALL POTS

1 kg (2 lb 4 ozs) kumquats
1.4 L (2½ pints/6 cups) water
140 ml (¼ pint/¾ cup) water (to cover seeds)
sugar
3 tablesp. (4 American tablesp.) Grand Marnier

Wash the kumquats, cut them into quarters and remove the seeds. Put the seeds into a small bowl, cover with 140 ml (¼ pint/¾ cup) cold water and leave overnight. Put the quartered kumquats into a larger bowl (not aluminium), cover with 1.4 L (2½ pints/6 cups) water and leave them overnight in a cool place.

Next day put the kumquats and their water into a stainless steel saucepan and strain the water off the seeds into the saucepan (press out every last drop because this water contains lots of pectin to help the jam to set). Bring it to the boil, cover and simmer for 45 minutes to 1 hour or until the rind is absolutely soft. Then measure the mixture and add an equal volume of sugar (1 cup sugar for every cup of cooked fruit). Heat the sugar in a moderate oven, 180°C/350°F/regulo 4, for about 10 minutes so that it will dissolve faster in the jam. When the sugar is hot to the touch, add it to the hot kumquats. Stir until all the sugar is dissolved, increase the heat and boil until the jam will set, 10–20 minutes approx. A blob of jam put on a cold saucer should wrinkle when pressed with the finger. Allow to stand for about 5 minutes, stir in the Grand Marnier, pour into sterilised jars and seal.

This delicious jam is expensive to make, so one might like to pot it into small jars rather than 450 g (1 lb) pots. The Grand Marnier is not absolutely essential.

Chocolate Christmas Tree

We had the greatest fun testing this recipe; it was Fionnuala's pride and joy and she was so proud of the result that she wouldn't let us sample it for several weeks. It still tasted delicious then, so it could be made well in advance of Christmas. Children could made it with a little adult supervision.

500 g (1 lb 2 ozs) best-quality dark chocolate
100 g (3½ ozs /⅔ cup) whole almonds, peeled and roasted
100 g (3½ ozs /⅔ cup) hazelnuts, peeled and roasted
50 g (1¾ ozs/⅓ cup) raisins
85–110 g (3–4 ozs) dark chocolate for assembling the tree
3 teasp. (1 American tablesp.) icing sugar

Decoration
Christmas cake decorations, e.g. Santa, robin, holly etc.

Drop the almonds into a saucepan of boiling water and boil for 2 minutes or until the skins loosen; drain. Put the almonds into a tea-towel, gather up the edges tightly and rub the almonds to get off the skins. Spread out on a baking sheet and bake in a moderate oven, 180°C/350°F/regulo 4, until dry and golden, 15 minutes approx. Meanwhile, spread the hazelnuts on another tray and bake in a hot oven, 230°C/450°F/regulo 8, for 15 minutes approx. until the skins loosen. Rub off the skins in a tea-towel in the same way as the almonds, return to the oven and bake until golden, about 15–20 minutes.

Prepare the trays to make the branches of the tree. Cover 3 baking trays or large Swiss roll tins with tin foil. Draw out crosses on the foil. Leave 5 or 7.5 cm (2 or 3 inches) between each cross. The measurements of the crosses are: 7 cm (2¾ inches), 9 cm (3½ inches), 11 cm (4¼ inches), 13 cm (5¼ inches), 14 cm (5¾ inches), 15 cm (6 inches), 16 cm (6½ inches), 17 cm (6¾ inches).

Prepare a serving plate for the tree: it must be rigid, absolutely flat and strong enough to support the tree. Cover with tin foil. Mark one of the 17 cm (6¾ inches) crosses on this base.

When the nuts are all golden, allow to cool and chop roughly. Mix with the raisins. When all the preparation is done, melt the chocolate very carefully in a very low oven or in a pyrex bowl over a saucepan of simmering water. Stir in the nuts and raisins, mix well. Using a teaspoon, drop small teaspoons of the chocolate mixture along the marked crosses (do the base board first and put in the fridge to set while you do the others, in order of size from the biggest to the smallest). When all the crosses have set absolutely firmly (30 minutes approx.), melt the remaining chocolate over a low heat. Put a teaspoon of melted chocolate onto the centre of the cross on the base board, and stick the next largest cross on top so that the points are in between the points of the previous cross.

While that is setting (supported with a matchbox if necessary), drop another teaspoon of chocolate on top of the second cross to form a basis for the next layer. Refrigerate for a few minutes. Meanwhile stick the remaining 8 crosses together in pairs in the same way and allow to set. Add another teaspoon of melted chocolate and put the next largest pair of crosses on top, angling them so the branches are arranged alternately. Continue to assemble until the tree is finished, however do it gradually: it is essential that each section is completely set before topping with another layer.

To serve: Decorate the board with Christmas decorations and dust the tree lightly with sieved icing sugar.

Mary Jo's Chocolates

MAKES 50 APPROX.

Even though these home-made chocolates are a little fiddly to make, believe me when you taste them you will reckon it was worth every minute!

225 g (8 ozs) best-quality dark chocolate
285 ml (½ pint/1¼ cups) cream
½–1 tablesp. (2–4 American teasp.) rum *or* orange liqueur

For coating the chocolates
225 g (8 ozs) best-quality dark chocolate
2 tablesp. (8 American teasp.) tasteless oil

Put the cream in a heavy-bottomed, preferably stainless steel saucepan and bring it almost to the boil. Remove from the heat and add the chopped chocolate. With a wooden spoon, stir the chocolate into the cream until it is completely melted. Transfer the chocolate cream to the bowl of a food mixer and allow it to cool to room temperature. Add the liqueur and whisk until it is just stiff enough to pipe. Using a piping bag and an 8 mm (⅜ inch) plain nozzle, pipe the mixture into small blobs onto a tray lined with silicone paper. Smooth top of the chocolates with your finger or better still a teaspoon dipped regularly in iced water! Put the tray in the fridge to allow the chocolates to set.

Meanwhile gently melt 225 g (8 ozs) chocolate for coating the chocolates, stir in 2 tablesp. (8 American teasp.) tasteless oil — either peanut or sunflower are best. When the chocolates have become quite cool, with the help of 2 forks dip them into the melted chocolate and coat them evenly. Place on a wire tray and allow to set. The chocolates are now ready to be served or may be decorated further by dribbling the tops with more melted chocolate.

Store in a covered container in a cool place. They are best eaten on the same day, but will in fact keep for 3 or 4 days.

Chocolate Fruit and Nuts

MAKES 35 APPROX.

225 g (8 ozs) best-quality dark chocolate
110 g (4 ozs/¾ cup) plump raisins
110 g (4 ozs/¾ cup) hazelnuts
30 g (1 oz) candied orange peel (preferably home-made, see page 90)

Put the hazelnuts into a moderate oven, 180°C/350°F/regulo 4, for 15–20 minutes or until the skins loosen. Remove from the oven and rub off the skins in a tea-towel. Return the skinned hazelnuts to the oven and toast until golden. Cool and cut in half. Cut the candied orange peel in 3 mm (⅛ inch) dice. Melt the chocolate carefully in a bowl over simmering water or in a *very* low oven. Stir the toasted hazelnuts, raisins and candied peel into the chocolate. Cover a tray or baking sheet with silicone paper and drop little heaps of the mixture neatly onto the paper from a small teaspoon. Don't make them too large because this mixture is quite rich. Tidy them up a little if necessary.

Allow to set hard in a cold place, preferably not in the fridge or they will lose their sheen. When set, peel them off the paper and put them into brown chocolate paper cases. Pack them into a pretty box or basket.

Chocolate Truffles

MAKES 25

Chocolate Truffles are irresistible and make very acceptable presents; eat them within a few days of making.

---

110 g (4 ozs) best-quality dark chocolate
1 tablesp. (4 American teasp.) cold water
30 g (1 oz/⅛ cup) castor sugar
85 g (3 ozs/¾ stick) unsalted butter
1 egg yolk
cocoa powder *and/or* very fine praline powder (see page 52)

Put the chocolate, water, butter and castor sugar into a heavy saucepan and melt on the lowest possible heat. Cool slightly and whisk in the egg yolk. Leave in a cool place to set and solidify for 4 or 5 hours, then shape into balls (bigger than a hazelnut, smaller than a walnut!). Roll the truffles in cocoa powder and/or finely ground praline powder. Put into paper cases.

Doreen's Fudge

MAKES 96 x 2.5 CM (1 INCH) SQUARES

Fudge is my father-in-law's absolute favourite after-dinner treat, so I had to include this recipe. I always used to be 'jinxed' when making fudge: it didn't seem to matter what recipe I tried, I could make a mess of it. However a lovely lady from Moyard, Co. Galway, called Doreen Linton gave me this recipe a few years ago; she swore it was fool-proof and indeed it must be because it works wonderfully for me — and it's also got my father-in-law's seal of approval!

225 g (8 ozs/2 sticks) butter
450 g (1 lb/scant 2¼ cups) castor sugar
1 tablesp. golden syrup
1 tin x 400 g (14 ozs/¾ cup) sweetened condensed milk
1 teasp. vinegar
1 teasp. pure vanilla essence

1 x 26.5 cm (10½ inches) x 18 cm (7 inches) tin

We use an 18 cm (7 inches) heavy-bottomed stainless steel saucepan. Brush the tin with some tasteless oil. Melt the butter with the castor sugar and syrup. Simmer for 5 minutes, add the condensed milk, bring to the boil again and simmer gently for 20 minutes, stirring all the time until it turns a rich golden brown. Remove from the heat and beat in the vinegar and vanilla essence. Pour into the oiled tin and cut into 2.5 cm (1 inch) squares.

Fudge will keep for a week in a tin, possibly even longer, but it has never been around that long!

Marzipan Dates
MAKES 28

Use up your scraps of almond paste on these Marzipan Dates.

28 fresh dates
110 g (4 ozs) almond paste *or* marzipan
castor sugar

Split one side of the date and remove the stone. Roll a little piece of marzipan into an oblong shape so that it will fit neatly into the opening. Smooth the top and roll the stuffed date in castor sugar. Repeat the procedure until all the dates and marzipan are used up. Serve as a petit four or as part of a selection of home-made sweets.

Orange, Lemon and Grapefruit Marmalade
YIELD 4.5 KG (10 LBS) APPROX.

Home-made marmalade is always a welcome present, particularly at Christmas, because quite often people have just run out of the previous year's marmalade. Seville oranges don't arrive into the shops until the end of January, so make this tangy 3-fruit marmalade in the meantime. It is made from orange, lemon and grapefruit, so may be made at any time of year.

2 sweet oranges and 2 grapefruit, weighing 1.35 kg (3 lbs) altogether
4 lemons
3.4 L (6 pints/14½ cups) water
2.7 kg (6 lbs/14¾ cups) sugar

Wash the fruit, cut in half and squeeze out the juice. Cut the peel in quarters and slice the rind across rather than lengthways. Put the juice, sliced rind and water in a bowl.

Put the pips in a muslin bag and add to the bowl. Leave overnight. The following day, simmer in a stainless steel saucepan with the bag of pips for 1½–2 hours until the peel is really soft. (Cover for the first hour.) The liquid should be reduced to about one-third of its original volume. Then remove the muslin bag, add the warmed sugar and stir until it has all dissolved; boil until it reaches setting point, about 8–10 minutes. Pour into sterilised jars and cover while hot.

Note: If the sugar is added before the rind is really soft, the rind will harden and no amount of boiling will soften it.

Pamelas

This is a most delicious way of using up left-over grapefruit peel. Properly candied, Pamelas will keep for several weeks in a screw-top jar.

4 pink *or* regular grapefruit
450 g (1 lb/2 cups) sugar
115 ml (4 fl ozs/½ cup) water
castor sugar

With a stainless steel knife, cut the tops and bottoms off the grapefruit, then cut off the peel down as far as the flesh. Cut the peel into pieces 6.5 x 1 cm (2½ x ½ inches) approx. Put the strips of peel into a stainless steel saucepan and cover with *cold* water, bring to the boil and boil for 2 minutes. Strain off all the water. Repeat the blanching twice more, using cold water each time to draw out the bitterness from the skins.

Meanwhile dissolve the sugar in water, bring to the boil, add the drained grapefruit peel and cook slowly until it becomes translucent, 30 minutes approx. Remove to a wire rack with a draining spoon. Allow to dry and cool, then toss in castor sugar. Serve as a petit four or as part of a selection of home-made sweets.

Home-made Candied Peel

5 oranges
5 lemons
5 grapefruit
or all of one fruit
1.35 kg (3 lbs/6 cups) sugar
water
1 teasp. salt

Cut the fruit in half and squeeze out the juice. Reserve the juice for another use, perhaps Home-made Lemonade (see page 73). Put the peel into a large bowl (not aluminium), add salt and cover with cold water. Leave to soak for 24 hours. Next day throw away the soaking water, put the peel in a saucepan and cover with fresh cold water. Bring to the boil and simmer very gently until the peel is soft, 3 hours approx. Remove the peel and discard the water. Scrape out any remaining flesh and membranes from inside the cut fruit, leaving the white pith and rind intact.

Dissolve the sugar in 850 ml (1½ pints/3¾ cups) water, bring it to the boil, add the peel and simmer gently until it looks translucent, 30 minutes approx. Remove the peel, drain and leave it to cool. Boil down the remaining syrup until it becomes thick and syrupy but before it turns to a caramel. Remove from the heat and put the peel in again to soak up the syrup. Leave for 30 minutes.

Fill the candied peel into sterilised glass jars and pour the syrup over, cover and store in a cold place or in a fridge. Alternatively, cool the peel on a wire rack and pour any remaining syrup into the centres. Finally pack into sterilised glass jars and cover tightly. It should keep for 6–8 weeks or longer under refrigeration.

Palestrina Christmas Cake

Pan Giallo di Palestrina, a speciality of the Rome area
MAKES 10 LITTLE CAKES

A wonderful Italian cook called Ada Parasiliti from Milan taught me how to make these delicious cakes when she came to teach at the Ballymaloe Cookery School in 1986. They are packed solid with fruit and keep for a year or more — I discovered this because I put some away in a tin and forgot about them, then found them over a year later, still perfect. However it is absolutely essential to use best-quality dried fruit, fresh nuts and home-made or best-quality candied peel for this recipe.

355 g (12½ ozs/2½ cups) almonds
355 g (12½ ozs/2½ cups) hazelnuts
355 g (12½ ozs/3 generous cups) walnuts
355 g (12½ ozs/2 generous cups) raisins
155 g (5½ ozs/1 cup) pine nuts
100 g (3½ ozs) dark chocolate
100 g (3½ ozs/½ cup) candied orange peel (preferably home-made)
370 g (13 ozs/1¼ cup) best-quality Irish honey
the zest of 1 orange
the peel of 1 lemon
285 g (10 ozs/2 cups) approx. flour
355 g (12½ ozs /1¾ cups) sugar

Soak the raisins in hot water for a few hours and then drain on a cotton tea-towel. Peel and roast the almonds in a moderate oven for 20 minutes. Roast the hazelnuts, rub off the skins and return to the oven until pale golden.

In a heavy saucepan bring the honey and sugar to the boil with the grated orange and lemon peel. Add the almonds, stirring for 5 minutes approx. until they become golden. Next add the hazelnuts and mix for a few more minutes, then the pine nuts, walnuts, raisins, candied orange peel and chocolate. Mix all the ingredients well. Gradually sprinkle the flour into the mixture and cook for 10 minutes approx., stirring constantly.

Put 10 mounds of flour onto a clean work top, with the help of 2 wooden spoons; divide the mixture in 10 heaps on the flour. Wet your hands and then shape the mixture into small loaves. Place on several buttered baking sheets, and cook for 2–3 hours.

Preheat the oven to 170°C/325°F/regulo 3, and bake for 20–25 minutes approx. Immediately they come out of the oven, adjust the shape with a wet knife; allow them to get cold, wrap and store for one month to mature.

Serve thinly sliced.

CHRISTMAS BISCUITS

Ginger Christmas Tree Biscuits
MAKES 80 APPROX., DEPENDING ON THE SIZE OF THE CUTTER

110 g (4 ozs/½ cup) Barbados sugar (moist, soft, dark-brown sugar)
110 g (4 ozs/⅓ cup) black treacle
1 teasp. ground cinnamon
1 teasp. ground ginger
a pinch of ground cloves
85 g (3 ozs/¾ stick) butter
1½ teasp. (1½ American teasp.) baking powder
450 g (1 lb/3 cups) flour
a pinch of salt
1 egg

To decorate
225 g (8 ozs/1 generous cup) glacé or royal icing (optional) (see page 64)

Melt the butter, treacle, Barbados sugar and spices in a heavy-bottomed saucepan on a low heat. Stir until the sugar dissolves. Cool. Lightly beat in the egg. Sieve the flour, baking powder and salt into a bowl, make a well in the centre and pour in the beaten eggs and the cool treacle mixture. Stir very carefully from the centre to incorporate the flour gradually. Turn the mixture out onto a lightly-floured work top and knead for a minute or so until smooth. Cover with cling-film and leave to rest in a fridge for a minimum of 30 minutes.

Preheat the oven to 160°C/325°F/regulo 3.

Roll out the dough 3 mm (⅛ inch) approx. thick. Cut it into assorted shapes — stars, Christmas trees, hearts, Santas and gingerbread people. Transfer to a baking sheet. Make a hole near the top of each biscuit with a skewer. Bake for 8–10 minutes. Cool on a wire rack.

Decorate the gingerbread men and women with glacé icing and store in an airtight tin until needed. These biscuits will keep in an airtight tin for several weeks. Thread thin red or green ribbons through the hole in each biscuit and hang them on the Christmas tree.

Holy Biscuits

Hildabrotchen (Irene Bauer)

MAKES 45–50 APPROX.

310 g (11 ozs/2 generous cups) flour
150 g (generous 5 ozs/1¼ sticks) cold butter
120 g (generous 4 ozs/½ cup) vanilla castor sugar
1 egg

Filling
1–2 tablesp. (4–8 American teasp.) home-made raspberry jam (*Simply Delicious*, page 76)

To glaze
125 g (4½ ozs/scant 1 cup) icing sugar
1–2 dessertsp. (2–4 American teasp) hot water *or* alternatively, just dust with sieved icing sugar

Sieve the flour onto a clean work top, cut the butter into tiny bits and toss in flour so they won't stick together. Add the vanilla castor sugar and slightly-beaten egg and work it together quickly until it forms a dough. Cover with cling-film and leave to rest in a fridge for 1 hour approx.

Preheat the oven to 160°C/325°F/regulo 3.

Roll out the dough into a thin sheet 5 mm (¼ inch) approx. thick, stamp out into 5 cm (2 inches) diameter biscuits. Cut a tiny hole out of the centres of half of the biscuits using a 2.5 cm (1 inch) cutter. Bake for 25–30 minutes approx. Allow to get cold on a wire rack. Meanwhile, mix the icing sugar with a little boiling water to make a water icing.

To assemble: Spread a very little jam on the whole biscuits and top with the 'holy' biscuits, then ice the edges carefully. Alternatively, just dredge the 'holy' halves of the biscuits with icing sugar before sticking them onto the jam.

These biscuits may be stored in an airtight tin for several weeks.

Irene's 'S' Biscuits
(Irene Bauer)

MAKES 70 APPROX.

400 g (14 ozs/scant 3 cups) flour
255 g (9 ozs/2¼ sticks) butter
125 g (4½ ozs/generous ½ cup) castor sugar
6 egg yolks

Glaze
2 egg yolks
coarse sugar

Sieve the flour onto a clean work top, cut the butter into tiny cubes and toss them in the flour so they won't stick together. Make a well in the centre and put in the castor sugar and egg yolks. Pinch with your fingers and bring the mixture quickly together into a ball. Cover with cling-film and leave to rest in a fridge for 30 minutes. If the mixture is soft enough it can be piped through a small rose pipe into 'S' shapes; otherwise break off pieces, roll them into strips about as thick as your little finger, and then form into 'S' shapes. Put them onto a baking sheet which has been covered with silicone paper. Allow to rest in a cool place for about 30 minutes. Brush them carefully with slightly-beaten egg yolk and sprinkle with coarse sugar.

Preheat the oven to 160°C/325°F/regulo 3.

Bake in the preheated oven until barely golden, 20–25 minutes approx. Remove to a wire rack to cool.

These biscuits may be stored in an airtight tin for several weeks.

Checkerboard or Pinwheel Biscuits

MAKES 30 APPROX.

These biscuits are great fun to make.

Plain mixture
110 g (4 ozs/1 stick) butter
55 g (2 ozs/generous ¼ cup) castor sugar
170 g (6 ozs/scant 1 cup) flour

Chocolate mixture

110 g (4 ozs/1 stick) butter

55 g (2 ozs/generous ¼ cup) castor sugar

170 g (6 ozs/scant 1 cup) flour

30 g (2 tablesp./¼ cup) drinking chocolate powder

½ teasp. vanilla essence

a little beaten egg

Cover 2 baking sheets with silicone paper. Make both mixtures in the same way but in different bowls. (Add the essence with the dry ingredients to the chocolate mixture.) Put the dry ingredients into a bowl and rub the butter in until it all comes together into a ball. Rest both mixtures for 15–20 minutes in a fridge.

For Checkerboard Biscuits: Divide both chocolate and plain dough into 5 pieces each. You will have 10 pieces. Keep the biggest plain one aside, arrange one on top of the other in a checkerboard. Roll out the remaining piece into an oblong and wrap it around the role, seal the edges with a little beaten egg, chill in a fridge for 15–20 minutes or until firm enough to cut.

Preheat the oven to 180°C/350°F/regulo 4.

Cut the roll into 5 mm (¼ inch) slices, arrange on a baking sheet and bake for 20–25 minutes or until golden. Cool on a wire rack.

For Pinwheel Biscuits: Roll out both mixtures into a rectangle about 5 mm (¼ inch) thick, trim the edges, neatly lay one piece on top of the other and roll into a long Swiss Roll. Wrap in cling-film and chill in a fridge for 15–20 minutes or until firm enough to cut.

Preheat the oven to 180°C/350°F/regulo 4.

Cut the roll into 5 mm (¼ inch) slices, arrange on a baking sheet and bake in a preheated oven for 20–25 minutes or until golden.

These biscuits may be stored in an airtight tin for several weeks.

Butter Biscuits

Buttergebad (Irene Bauer)

MAKES 60–70 BISCUITS APPROX.

400 g (14 ozs/3½ sticks) butter
200 g (7 ozs/1 cup) sugar
5 egg yolks
500 g (1 lb 2 ozs/3⅔ cups) flour

Glaze
1 egg yolk
a tiny drop of cream

Line some baking sheets with silicone paper. Cream the butter and add the castor sugar and egg yolks. Beat until light and fluffy. Sieve and stir in the flour, turn out onto a board and knead the mixture until it comes together. Rest for 30 minutes approx. in a fridge.

Preheat the oven to 160°C/325°F/regulo 3.

Roll out to scant 5 mm (¼ inch) approx. thick, and stamp out into Christmas shapes, e.g. stars, moons, Christmas trees, Santas, etc. Put on a baking sheet and bake for 15–20 minutes approx. Cool on a wire tray.

These biscuits will keep for several weeks stored in an airtight tin.

Vanilla Moons

Vanilla Kipferl (Elsa Schiller)

MAKES 50 APPROX.

255 g (9 ozs/1¾ cups) flour
70 g (2½ ozs/scant ½ cup) castor sugar
110 g (4 ozs/1 generous cup) ground almonds
200 g (7 ozs/1¾ sticks) butter

For dusting
450 g (1 lb/4 cups) icing sugar
3 teasp. pure vanilla essence

Cover 2 baking sheets with silicone paper. Put the flour, castor sugar and ground almonds into a bowl, rub in the butter and squeeze together until the mixture forms a dough. Cover with cling-film and leave to rest for 30 minutes in a fridge.

Preheat the oven to 160°C/325°F/regulo 3.

Take off small pieces of dough about the size of a small walnut and form into half-moon shapes. Alternatively, roll out the dough onto a sheet 1 cm (½ inch) approx. thick. Cut in half-moons with a pastry cutter. Transfer onto a baking sheet and bake until pale golden in the preheated oven. Meanwhile, mix 3 teaspoons of vanilla essence into the icing sugar, then push through a sieve. Cover a Swiss roll tin with half of the sugar and put the hot biscuits onto the sugar; sieve the remainder of the icing sugar over them. Shake off the excess. Cool on a wire rack.

These biscuits will keep for several weeks stored in an airtight tin.

Note: Keep the left-over vanilla-flavoured icing sugar to sieve over fruit tarts or pies.

Rum Hearts
Rumherzen (Elsa Schiller)
MAKES 50–100, DEPENDING ON THE SIZE OF HEART-SHAPED CUTTER

500 g (1 lb 2 ozs/scant 3¾ cups) flour
2 level teasp. (1 American teasp.) baking powder
200 g (7 ozs/1 cup) castor sugar
2 eggs
1 teasp. pure vanilla essence
95 ml (3 tablesp./¼ cup) rum
a few drops of pure almond essence
finely-grated rind of 1 lemon
255 g (9 ozs/2¼ sticks) butter
200 g (7 ozs/2 cups) ground almonds

Icing
450 g (1 lb/4 cups) icing sugar
50–75 ml (4–5 tablesp./¼–½ cup) approx. rum

Decoration
50–100 split almonds

Cover 3 or 4 baking sheets with silicone paper (or bake in batches). Sieve the flour and baking powder into a bowl or onto a clean work top, add the ground almonds and castor sugar and mix well together. Cut the butter into small dice and rub into the flour and almonds. Whisk the eggs lightly and mix with the essences, rum and lemon rind. Add to the dry ingredients and mix to make a smooth dough. Cover with cling-film and leave to rest in the fridge for 1–2 hours if possible.

Preheat the oven to 160°C/325°F/regulo 3.

Roll the dough 5 mm (¼ inch) approx. thick, cut into heart shapes, transfer onto the baking sheets and bake in the preheated oven for 12–15 minutes or until golden. Meanwhile, mix the sieved icing sugar with enough rum to make a firm icing. When the hearts are cooked, remove them to a wire rack. While they are still hot, brush with the icing and stick a half almond in the centre of each one.

These biscuits may be stored in an airtight tin for several weeks.

Almond Crisps
MAKES 30 BISCUITS

110 g (4 ozs/1 cup) self-raising flour
55 g (2 ozs/¼ cup) castor sugar
55 g (2 ozs/½ stick) butter
2 egg yolks
a pinch of salt

Icing
110 g (4 ozs/½ cup) icing sugar
1 egg white

To decorate
45 g (1½ ozs /⅓ cup) roughly-chopped almonds

Cover 2 baking sheets with silicone paper. Sieve the flour and salt into a bowl and add the castor sugar. Rub in the butter until the mixture resembles coarse crumbs. Add the egg yolks and mix to a firm dough. Wrap and chill for 30 minutes.

Preheat the oven to 180°C/350°F/regulo 4.

Roll out the pastry on a lightly-floured work top or between 2 pieces of greaseproof paper. Cut the pastry with a floured 5 cm (2 inches) round fluted cutter. Place the biscuits on the prepared baking sheets.

To make the icing, whisk the egg white to the soft peak stage and gradually add in the icing sugar. Put a small teaspoon of icing in the centre of each biscuit, smooth it slightly and sprinkle the chopped almonds on top of the biscuits. Bake in the preheated oven for 15–18 minutes or until a light golden brown. Cool on a wire rack.

These biscuits may be stored in an airtight tin for up to 2 weeks.

Almond Macaroons

(Irene Bauer)

MAKES 50

255 g (9 ozs/scant 2 cups) skinned dry whole almonds
3 egg whites
255 g (9 ozs/scant 1¼ cups) castor sugar
rind of ½ lemon

For the top
18 almonds split in half

Preheat the oven to 130°C/250°F/regulo ½.

Cover 2 or 3 baking sheets with silicone paper. Drop the whole almonds into boiling water, bring back to the boil for 1 or 2 minutes or until the skins loosen, drain and rub off the skins in a tea-towel. Put in a Swiss roll tin into a low oven for 5–10 minutes to allow them to dry out well. Grind to a gritty powder in a food processor or liquidiser. Whisk the egg whites with the castor sugar until very stiff, fold in the almonds and a little lemon rind. Drop little blobs on the baking sheets. Top each with half an almond. Bake in the preheated oven for 40 minutes approx. or until they peel off the paper. Cool on a wire rack.

These biscuits may be stored in an airtight tin for 2–3 weeks.

Coconut Macaroons

(Irene Bauer)

MAKES 60 APPROX.

4 egg whites
255 g (9 ozs/1¼ cups) vanilla castor sugar
170 g (6 ozs/scant 2 cups) desicated coconut

Preheat the oven to 150°C/300°F/regulo 2.

Cover 2 or 3 baking sheets with silicone paper. Whisk the egg whites with the vanilla sugar until very stiff and fold in the dessicated coconut gently. Drop teaspoons of the mixture onto the baking sheets and bake in the preheated oven for 40 minutes approx. Cool on a wire rack.

These biscuits may be stored in an airtight tin for 3–4 weeks.

This mixture also makes two 18 cm (7 inch) meringue discs which can be sandwiched together with chunks of fresh pineapple and cream.

Hazelnut Macaroons
(Irene Bauer)
MAKES 50 APPROX.

255 g (9 ozs/scant 2 cups) grated hazelnuts
255 g (9 ozs/1¼ cups) vanilla castor sugar
4 egg whites

For the top
50 whole toasted hazelnuts

Preheat the oven to 190°C/375°F/regulo 5.

Roast the 50 hazelnuts for 15–20 minutes or until the skins loosen, remove from the oven and rub off the skins in a tea-towel, then return to the oven for 15–20 minutes or until golden. Cover 2 or 3 baking sheets with silicone paper. Whisk the egg stiffly with the castor sugar until they hold a stiff peak. Fold in the grated hazelnuts. Drop a teaspoon of the mixture onto the baking sheets and top each one with a toasted hazelnut. Bake in the preheated oven for 40 minutes approx. Cool on a wire rack.

These biscuits may be stored in an airtight tin for 2–3 weeks.

Hazelnut Sticks
(Irene Bauer)
MAKES 45 APPROX.

140 g (5 ozs/1 cup) flour
125 g (4½ ozs/1⅛ sticks) cold butter
125 g (4½ ozs/½ cup) vanilla castor sugar
125 g (4½ ozs/1 cup) ground hazelnuts

Glaze
1 egg white
85 g (3 ozs/¾ cup) icing sugar

Sieve the flour onto a clean work top, cut the cold butter into tiny pieces and toss in flour so they won't stick together. Mix in the ground hazelnuts and vanilla castor sugar and knead until it forms a dough. Cover and leave to rest in a fridge for 1 hour.

Preheat the oven to 150°C/300°F/regulo 2.

Meanwhile, line 2 or 3 baking sheets with silicone paper. Roll out the dough 5 mm (¼ inch) thick and cut into strips 2 cm (¾ inch) wide and 7.5 cm (3 inches) long; transfer onto the baking sheets. Whisk the egg white lightly and stir in the icing sugar. Spread a little glaze on each biscuit with a knife. Bake for 20 minutes approx. Cool on a wire rack.

These biscuits may be stored for 3 to 4 weeks in an airtight tin.

Index